GIN CITY

WRITING FROM PLYMOUTH

EDITED BY JON MACKLEY AND NICK INGRAM

CONTENTS

INTRODUCTION

This is the first volume in a new initiative which brings together work from both established and up-and-coming writers and artists, providing a new platform for their work. This volume contains some of the very best of poetry and prose coming out of the city of Plymouth – the Gin City. It brings together a variety of unique and exciting voices in contemporary poetry and prose that deserve to be heard and demand publication. Evocative, provocative, poignant, political, nostalgic, and sometimes addressing challenging issues close to the authors' hearts: there is something here for everyone.

The editors are grateful to all the contributors who have worked with us – poets, prose writers and artists – who have submitted their work for consideration in the first instance and worked with us on returning the proofs in good time.

If you enjoy the work in this volume then please let others know about the Gin City project. Please also support the authors by looking for their other work or follow to see if they are performing at any live events.

If you have any enquiries or would like to be involved in future publications then please contact the editors at Gincityplymouth@yahoo.com or look for details on the website at www.jonmackley.wixsite.com/gin-city

Jon Mackley   Nick Ingram

CHARLES BECKER

KITTY RAWLINS AND THE ARCHANGEL SPENCE

Yes, well, those were exciting times back then 'Course I was a young man with a young man's sense of invincibility. Only I wasn't invincible to the charms of a pretty woman. No, sir, I certainly wasn't invincible to those.
I remember the day Kitty Rawlins walked into my life. What a looker she was! Tall and straight as a poplar, with melt-your-heart dark brown eyes the size of saucers and a smile as wide as Canada. Just light you up in a flash.

I was dealin' with devils at the time, with the torments of drink and empty pockets.

I heard the rustle of her dress first and then her voice: "Why's a man like you sleeping rough in the street?"

Her words flowed over me like honey, as she stretched out a hand and pulled me to my feet. "That's better! You certainly look more dignified standing up."

I didn't know if I was being admired or acmonished.

I only know I caught the whiff of gardenias as I came up level with her. She had kind of sharp features, all cheekbones and jaw and coils of hair pinned up. Reminded me of a school teacher, but she sure was pretty.

"What's your name?" she asked me.

"Spence," I told her.

"Well, Spence…" She paused. "What kind of a name is that, anyway?"

"Only one I got," I said.

That's when her face split into this great gash of a smile; and, what with the glitter in her eyes and the shine off her teeth, I thought she was about to have me for her supper.

"Never mind," she says. "Spence it is and we're going to have a talk about your rehabilitation."

"I'm fine happy with this habitation right here," I tell her. "I like being out in the open."

She just laughs and says, "Tell you what, Spence, see that cafe over there? We're going to go in there and I'm going to buy you breakfast fit for a horse."

Sounded like some infernal hell of the damned, when we walked in, like being smacked in the face by a west coast roller; folks jabbering, waitresses calling, trays banging, knives and forks striking on china, chefs hollerin' and a coffee machine building up steam like a locomotive.

Boy, I'm tellin' you, if that whole buildin' had taken off across country, wouldn't have surprised me one bit!

She led me through an arch to a table where it was quieter somewhat and talked all the while I ate. By the time I'd finished my eggs and fried potatoes and bacon and tomatoes and God knows what else, I was totally smitten. I couldn't take my eyes off her. I tell you, if the hog's puddin' had gone in my ear 'stead of my mouth, I wouldn't have noticed.

"So, that's the deal," she ended up. "What do you say?"

"Yes," is what I said, though I'd no idea what the deal were. I'd been too busy watching her mouth dimplin' at the corners as she spoke and wonderin' at the way stray strands of her hair went curlin' round her ears like petals round a bud.

'Course, I had no idea what I was lettin' myself in for. Force of nature that Kitty Rawlins. Certainly was. Force of nature, all right.

Spark came into her eyes, like a hunting dog on the scent, and we were off.

She had me shaved, barbered and bathed and then reclothed, before I'd had time to put the cap back on the ketchup.

"You're a fine-looking man under all that degradation," she said finally, appraising me out on the sidewalk.

Caught sight of myself in a store window and didn't know who I was looking at. Person in the reflection got nothing to do with the person inside me, I can tell you that.

"Aidycomp," she called me, whatever that means.

Well, I'd worked fairgrounds, games parks and racecourses too. I get along pretty well with horses. But I'd never been an escort before.

Deal turned out to be I was to accompany Ms Rawlins on her lecture tour. Drove her from town to town, big ones, little ones, didn't make no matter. Took the door at her rallies and made sure she got back safely to her room every night.

There were plenty of folks wanted to do her harm, once she opened up on poverty and deprivation and the need for equality, no matter where you come from or what the colour of your skin was. Said women were the most put upon of all and she wanted laws changed to give them equal rights with men, who were makin' all the rules.

Never had so many arguments and fist fights before or since. Husbands, businessmen, die-hards, even some starch-faced matrons, all came pilin' in. Had my nose broken twice and my jaw, ribs kicked in and enough black eyes to spot a leopard!

"Why are you being so provocative, Spence?" she would say, dabbin' at the cuts on me with some stingin' ointment of hers. "I never knew a man before with your inclination for getting into trouble."

And I'd get so all-fired riled up at the turn-around injustice of it that I could hardly get my words out. "It's you doin' all the provokin'!" I'd explode. "I'm just … I'm just lookin' out for you, all the time. So … so … Goddammit!"

Next thing, she'd be grinnin' and laughin' at me with so much evident delight, she took all the hurtin' and the anger out of me. And then she'd come in close, puttin' her face up to mine and fixin' me with those eyes of hers like sinkin' sand, you could fall right into them. Restin' the palm of her hand on me, "Spence," she'd say, soft as if someone had turned the volume down low, "you're my protector, my street angel." And she'd lift up on her toes and kiss me so lightly it felt like I'd got feathers on my lips … oh, boy! I'd tremble at the sweetness of her, I can feel it now. "You're my Michael and you're going to join the Archangels. Archangel Spence."

I didn't know if she was foolin' with me or fallin' in love with me. But I do know it sort of filled me out … as if everything was right with the world and with me. Gave me a sense of purpose and … I don't know … of a kind of goodness in myself. Yes, you could say that … yes, indeed.

Anyway, there I were, lookin' out for her, when one night in the middle of one of her speeches … don't remember where exactly … some meeting hall up north, maybe … a bunch of guys come burstin' in, wavin' clubs, just itchin' for a fight and yellin' out against her, callin' her a 'commie dyke' and tellin' her to 'take her tits back to the kitchen' and worse. And, in the commotion that followed, a stream of cops come pilin' in … helmets, riot shields, the lot … break up the meetin' and cart Kitty Rawlins away, arrestin' **her** for 'disturbin' the peace'.

When I started protestin' and tryin' to explain wasn't none of her fault, one of 'em slammed me with his truncheon and hauled me out to the van. Turned out he'd broken my collarbone and I ended up at the hospital.

She got three years in prison on some technical charge I never really understood, somethin' about underminin' the political and economic stability of the state. Didn't seem to dim her light none; told the judge he was 'a patriarchal dinosaur', which earned her an extra month for contempt.

They fined me a whole lotta money and I went back on the road, didn't want no more part of their world. Wrote to Kitty a few times, once I was someplace long enough to hear back from her. Her replies always came addressed to 'Archangel Spence'. But she got moved and I didn't know where. Besides, by that time, I'd gotten involved with a long distance truck driver, Della Riva; and I was happy enough for a time ridin' along with her, with her wild hair like a burning bush and legs as sturdy as the tree trunks she was haulin'.

Didn't last though, no more than any of the others. Somehow, my thoughts always went back to Kitty, like she'd carved her name in my brain. Middle of nowhere, there she'd be, fillin' my head, just standin' there, hands on hips, and grinnin' at me, scent of gardenias in the air.

Then, blow me, one day I'm fixin' some barn doors … had a small maintenance business at the time … when the farmer's wife comes over, tells me there's a phone call.

"Would that be the Archangel Spence, by any chance?" Her voice was deeper, but I'd have recognized the teasin' note to it anyplace. Damn near fell over with the shock of it.

"Kitty Rawlins!" I exploded. "Well, I … I …"

Just as well she cut short my stammerins, as I was pure lost for words, couldn't get my wits together.

"I see you've lost none of your eloquence," she says. "No matter. The thing is, Spence, I'm running for public office and I need someone I can trust."

'Course, I went. Dropped everythin'. Turned out campaignin' wasn't much different to lecturin', 'cept she got elected, not arrested. Did a lot of good things, too. Folks'll say I'm biased, no doubt, 'cause I stayed with her after that, all those years before the cancer got her. Never did marry her though. Wanted to. Proposed to her any number of times, but she'd just wink at me: "Archangels can't get married, Spence, can they?" And she'd put her arms round me and whirl me around in a dance, till she spun the idea right out of my head … until the next time, anyway.

When Caroline came back from her bedtime bath, she discovered her husband, George, propped up in bed reading a book with his faded, cotton cap on. It was the final straw and two days later she found herself opposite a pinched-face solicitor in a brown tie.

"So, to sum up, Mr Shruggs," she said, realizing her free 30 minutes were almost up, "I want to know if I can sue George for divorce on the grounds of the irretrievable breakdown of our marriage, due to his unreasonable behaviour in refusing to remove his cap in the house or even in the bedroom, as I have told you."

"Yeeeez," Mr Shruggs said on a prolonged outbreath; "unfortunately, as the law stands, you see, aesthetic abuse," he smiled thinly, "is not a recognized basis for such a proceeding."

Later the same day, Caroline was having tea with her friend, Molly. Molly, a patient, middle-aged woman, was cutting out bright red patches of material for the quilt she was making.

"What do you think?" she said, holding scarlet floral against turquoise abstract.

"The man's a fool!" Caroline said. "I told him about the boiler suit, as well, and he barely raised an eyebrow."

"You're right," Molly nodded, setting down her pinking shears and the scarlet patch, "maybe it is a bit garish."

Caroline brushed a biscuit crumb from her lap. "I've told you before, haven't I? He won't take the boiler suit off when he comes in, because of that bloody mouse!"

"Mouse?" Molly said. "I did a nursery quilt once with three blind mice. Couldn't find a farmer's wife or a knife, but used a milkman and chip pan instead."

"What on earth are you talking about?" Caroline demanded.

Molly beamed at her and started chanting: "They all ran after the milkman, who fried their tails in a chip pan."

"Oh, for goodness sake, Molly," Caroline broke in. "This is serious!"

Molly shrugged her becardiganed shoulders and went back to her snipping.

"The point is," Caroline continued, "George takes the anaemic, little beast to work in his top pocket and won't take off the wretched garment when he comes home, because … and it defies belief, it really does … he doesn't want to disturb 'dear Pinky'!"

"Pink and white are a bit wishy washy, don't you think?" Molly said, sifting through some remnants and drawing one out to illustrate her point.

"Pinky, I ask you!" The teaspoon jumped in Caroline's saucer, as she thumped her cup down. "Just because of its horrid little eyes. Disturb it, huh! I'll disturb it all right. Farmer's wife had the right idea. I'm telling you he thinks more of that mouse than he does of me. Well, I've had enough, I'm leaving him. And it's no use trying to talk me out of it, Molly; my mind's made up."

Molly extricated a roll of material from under the sofa and unfurled a length of it across the carpet. "What would you think of a whole quilt in dove grey with cucumber green fronds?"

When Caroline got home, she packed up the mid-grey, baker boy cap she had ordered in herringbone, which George had refused. "Makes me look like a Peaky Blinders' gunman," he'd told her. Well, her mother had warned her all those years ago. "N.O.C.D." she'd said, with a knowing smile. "Not our class, dear."

Caroline stuck the return label on the package and took it to the post office.

Coming along the path on her way home again, she saw her neighbour polishing his ancient car in his trilby.

"Afternoon, Leonard," she said, drawing level. "Outdoors is the proper place for a hat, if I may say so."

"So's a bald 'ead," he grinned.

She went to move on, but he put up his hand. "Hang on a minute, I've got something for 'ee." And leaving his cloth on the bonnet, he disappeared into his house.

"Dug 'er up this mornin'," he said, coming back and holding out a mud-spattered, purple and orange swede. "Go well in a stew for George, I reckon."

"We're having chicken casserole," she said, taking a plastic carrier from her bag. She shook it and held it open; and, as he dropped the vegetable in, her arms sagged with the weight of it.

"Some people confuse swedes with turnips." she went on. "I did once!"

She closed the handles and held the carrier by her side. "But swedes have proper substance, Leonard, and they don't wear caps in bed!"

As she walked off, Leonard pushed back his hat and scratched his head.

It was almost six o'clock when George came through the back door into the kitchen.

"Smells good," he said, putting his sandwich box on the side by the sink.

He moved forward to greet her with a peck on the cheek, as usual; but she stepped back from the chopping board, knife still in hand.

"Right," she said, "let's get this straight once and for all. You take that cap off and you go upstairs and change out of that boiler suit. I'm not going to put up with you being dressed in the house like that any longer."

As she spoke, pink eyes and a twitching, whiskered nose appeared over the rim of his top pocket.

"And I won't have that ... that rodent in the house anymore either. I mean it."

"Oh, come on, love, let it be," George sighed, turning for the door to the hall. "It's been a long day."

"Don't you turn your back on me, George Dodd!" She tossed the knife onto the table. "I want an answer and I want it now, or else we go our separate ways."

George turned round again to face her. "You're not serious, are you, love?" he said. "I mean, I don't 'ave to dress up in me own 'ome, do I?"

Caroline lifted her chin. "I've been to see a solicitor. Aesthetic abuse, he called it."

George shook his head. "I don't even know what that means," he muttered, glancing down at the mouse. Then, looking up at her again, he added: "I know you're ashamed of me sometimes and that you don't feel I'm good enough for you; but I am doing my best and I do lov ..."

The swede caught him high up on the side of his head, near the temple; and, as he went down, his head bounced on the tiled floor, his cap fell off, the mouse ran away, and Caroline knew it was the end.

Charlie Moon was a good sort, everybody said so. He might not be very bright, they said; but he was kindhearted and good with his hands. He worked for Tom Fisher's Carpet Warehouse, not far from the village, out on the new industrial estate. Charlie was one of their fitters and he was well-known, turning up in his transit van with rolls of carpet and underlay and his friendly grin.

Among the locals, he was often referred to affectionately as 'Boots', because of his tendency to trip going up stairs, catching the toe of one of his heavy boots on the lip of a step, and stumbling on. If they laughed with him, he was happy enough; but if he felt they were laughing at him, his jaw would go rigid and he'd close himself off, a thunder scowl darkening his face.

It seldom took long for the hurt to abate and the sun to come out again, however. And, when people ordered a carpet from Tom Fisher, they'd always double-checked that Charlie would be fitting it and not the other bloke, who was dour and uncommunicative and not at all 'handy'. The truth was people took advantage of Charlie Moon, when he came to their house. They'd mention the cupboard door that had 'gone wrong' and didn't close properly anymore and Charlie would offer to have a look at it, once he'd laid the carpet.

Mrs Deacon, from the bakery, mentioned the fox getting at her chickens and Charlie said he'd come round at the weekend and see what he could do. And he did. And he worked hard most of that Saturday putting in deeper, taller fencing for her.

"Did she pay you?" his wife asked when he got back.

He grinned at her sheepishly: "Yes … well, you know, for the materials."

"Oh, Charlie! What are we going to do with you?" Affection and exasperation filled her eyes and words. "Baby's coming soon. We need the money, love."

He reddened and glanced down at his boots, before looking back at her.

"A fox had got all her chickens. I couldn't ask for money, could I? I mean, I was just trying to help."

Sandra moved past the kitchen table and put her arms round him.

"Yes, I know, and you're lovely like that, but people take advantage of you. You go to fit a carpet and end up fixing their houses for them." She gave him a squeeze. "They'd have to pay anyone else, you know."

"Yes, but we ought to help each other without wanting money for it, shouldn't we? I mean that's what it's all about, isn't it?"

"You're God's own fool, Charlie Moon!" she said, letting go of him. She pulled round a chair and sat down, stretching out her legs and gently stoking her swollen belly. "There are things we're going to need for this little one. You don't have to ask a lot, just what's fair."

"You're right, you're right," he said, squatting down and closing his hand over hers and the baby. "That's what I'll do … I'll ask for what's fair."

But he never did. There never seemed to be a right moment; and, once he'd finished and the customer was beaming a smile of gratitude at him, he just couldn't find it in himself to ask.

The night Sandra died, everything went black, as if he'd fallen down a well and seen the light go out at the top. He didn't understand what he was told at the hospital. Was she a doctor? "Amniotic fluid embolism … cardio-respiratory collapse …" Didn't matter, anyway. Sandra and the baby were dead and nothing was going to change that.

Later on, his mother tried to explain it to him: "She had severe bleeding and the fluid round the baby got into her bloodstream … her heart and lungs failed." But, although he recognized the words, they didn't mean anything to him; and he went back to his two-bedroomed terraced house, wanting to be alone.

Most of the time, he sat in Sandra's armchair, with the lights off, staring at the window and the winter gloom beyond. Tom Fisher rang and told him to take as much time off as he needed. And Mrs Deacon called round with two carrier bags of shopping and a tray of eggs. "You look after yourself, Charlie," she said. "And, if there's anything I can do, you call me, all right?" After she'd gone, he left the bags and tray on the kitchen table; and, in the days that followed, he ignored the doorbell and the knocking.

There was rope in the garden shed and he thought about hanging himself from the upstairs banister into the hall; but he couldn't find the energy to move.

Late one afternoon, as he was sitting on the downstairs loo, the central heating cut in with a whoosh from the combi boiler and the blank oval eye in its white cabinet suddenly came alive, a blazing brilliant blue. He sat transfixed, losing himself in its purity and intensity. He felt connected, his isolation penetrated.

On impulse, he pulled up his trousers and rushed upstairs to their bedroom. Afraid the blue light might disappear in his absence, he grabbed the small, brass Buddha from his bedside table, the dark Mother Kali figure from Sandra's, and four more gods and goddesses from her dressing-table, before racing down the stairs again. Wonderfully, the blue eye was still glowing. He flipped the seat and sat down, depositing his treasure of small statues onto the laminated shelf under the boiler.

"They're all part of the same story," Sandra had told him. "It's just people see different bits and think that's the whole if it."

Her Aunt May had left her a china statue of the Virgin Mary, her head covered. She was dressed in a long blue robe, with a matching cloak edged in gold; and, in her arms, was the baby Jesus. Sandra kept the figure between her hairbrush and the mirror.

"I know she isn't," she would say to him, picking it up, "but, when I hold her, I feel like Aunty May is here with me."

Charlie leant forward and stood the Blessed Virgin slightly to the right below the blue eye. The only other one of similar height was a porcelain sculpture of the Hindu Goddess, Lakshmi. With her four arms and gilded halo, she was seated on a lotus flower; and he placed her to the left, correspondingly. He sat back and regarded them. "Purity and serene beauty," he heard Sandra saying; and she was right, their expressions were so similar they could have been sisters.

The four remaining icons were smaller and much of a size. He wondered how best to position them and decided to put the brass Buddha in the middle, a little in front of Mary and Lakshmi.

"To keep you safe from your nightmares," Sandra had told him, placing the smiling figure level with his pillow. And it had worked. Each night, he gazed at the legs folded in the lotus position and raised palms pressed together as if in prayer, then fell asleep with the Buddha's image sealed beneath his eyelids.

His hand wandered to the dark resin figure of Kali, Goddess of Death; and, as if studying her for the first time, wondered why, with her six arms wielding six swords, she hadn't given Sandra bad dreams. But Sandra's words came back to him, telling him why: "She's the warrior in me, keeping baby safe … keeping us all safe."

"Well, you didn't keep them bloody safe, did you, *Mother* Kali?" he cried out, banging it down to the left of the Buddha. The blue light disappeared. "Sorry … sorry," he stammered, staring at the dark, blank eye. He dropped his head, blaming himself and wanting to erase his angry words. "I'm sorry," he said again, looking up at Kali; but, eventually, it was in the faces of Mary and Lakshmi that he found the reassurance to continue.

"You look hopeful," he muttered, lifting the little bronze figure with a trunk and elephant's head, who was dancing on one leg. "Maybe, you can help me." He set Ganesh down on the other side of the Buddha.

The boiler whooshed and the eye flared into life again. Charlie smiled and sat back, the tension going out of him. Still lying on its back and, as yet, unplaced was a squat, stone statue. He reached out and wrapped his fingers around it, clasping it in his palm. It felt rough and dry. Maybe, it wasn't really stone. He closed his eyes and revolved it between his fingers, running the pad of his thumb over the smooth back and ridged, carved front.

He opened his eyes again. He wasn't sure where to put it. It didn't seem to go with the rest. He couldn't remember what Sandra had told him about this particular God. He unfurled his fingers and stared at the wide, flat face, with its letter-box mouth and four only teeth, two on each side. "You're quite ugly," he whispered. In a way, it reminded him of himself and he held onto it, slipping it into his pocket.

In the days and weeks that followed, first thing in the morning and again when he got home from work, he would close himself in the downstairs loo and sit in front of the little shrine of intermediaries, waiting for the divine eye to open to him.

"How are you and baby?" he would start, before going on to tell Sandra about his day

THOM BOULTON

I AM WHY YOUR GHOST NO LONGER SPEAKS

Naked
from Prima Materia, 2018

When I strip my clothes off
they become possessed — not air
a figure forms, the buttons
eye me and pass judgment

Milky blues squint to decide fate

Could my hair be unravelled
as a cotton wheel, loose from my
mother's wicker basket?

The sleeves go flat to break my back
slams, orders community service

They made a teacher out of me
by dyeing pound coins red
and slapping me in the face
with a fake, rolled up degree

Congratulations Mrs Boulton, it's a civil servant

The stitching in the shin of my jeans
reads through my CV
makes suggestions and labels
my measurements with bullet points
— sharp as poppers on a fly

I try, but the wigs and whips lacerate flesh
until steam escapes and fades my body

Hard times breaking rocks with your skull
— repeating the same questions with only doubt
ever bothering to reply

If God were real, I imagine him to be sat on the toilet
crushing silverfish under his shoes

As I strip bare I see marks on my arms
old scars and contours
I am unfamiliar with them

For the first time I know how many chest hairs I have
I know their names; meet all of their kids

I scold the material, now I am judge

Being naked, you feel the cold more
squirm at heat

you know what pigment is hiding beneath
how different it is
to the colouring and freckles others see

Fleeting
from Prima Materia, 2018

These pasty arms made of plaster
hold the imprint of your tiny body

shrivelled little thing

The hands remember the feel of rubber
— a ball of elastic bands folding into lumps

Your vernix coat, moisturiser
with a water-base, it washes away
but my mind refuses to
clean the memory with a towel

Could I make buds of it, scented
and stuff them up my nose
to block out the dreaded aroma of roses?

Gazing into pools of dribble
cobalt cries
that scratch the marrowbone clear out

Hollow bones for rattles
shredded nerves
in place of peas or dried rice

There is a nagging feeling
that soon, crow's feet
will not be the only pattering, and
learning to fly will shortly follow

I'll watch you float amongst the stars
Selene in orbit
with Leo stalking close behind

**Looking For Jeremy Corbyn On The
18.26 Great Western Railway Train From
Penzance to London Paddington.**
from Prima Materia, 2018

Looking for Jeremy Corbyn
on the 18.26 Great Western Railway train
from Penzance to London Paddington
calling at
St Austell, Par, Bodmin Parkway
Liskeard, Plymouth, Newton Abbot
Exeter St Davids, Taunton, Bristol Temple Meads
Bath Spa
Reading
and London Paddington

Eyes right
to see
conductor's buttocks
framed in a green coat

he's asking for tickets
he's asking a man for his ticket

"Excuse me."

The man has lids shut
and is resting his chin
loosely on his collar

"Old fella!"
"Excuse me."

Shit, he's dead
Shit, he's fucking dead

"Excuse me mate!"

A stir, a gasp
fish on a frying pan

he stares at me
with my pupils I
communicate

"I'm not Jeremy Corbyn.
Have you seen him?
I know he likes trains."

But the man just stares
then fumbles for his ticket

I now set regular vibrating alarms
using my wrist watch
I set them to stop me from falling asleep dead

Eyes forward
to see
two pink bobbles
atop another bobble
who is taking photos

she snaps
snap — snap — snap
she snaps a picture
of not a pout or pose
but a porous expression
leaking out how grim life is

she texts the picture
asking the soon to be recipient

'Will you be my boyfriend?'

She is not Jeremy Corbyn
(the girl taking serious selfies)
her soon to be boyfriend
isn't Jeremy Corbyn either

Eyes down
to see
a pair of swirly, whirly
red patterned boots
having a conversation
with two scraps
of tangerine peel

Their owner is holding
Tony Blair's face in her lap
stroking his
thin, page-boy hair
typing love letters to him
on her Macbook, making
an eHarmony profile to
cleverly seduce Tony Blair

She has his face in her lap
but she wants more
New Labour to be Nude Labour

saucy Tony Blair and his kinky wink
he's got those winky eyes

even on matted paper
even after photoshop

He looks at me through the gap in the chairs
and he uses his winky eyes to ask me

"Have you seen Jeremy Corbyn?
He
uses trains
and I thought, maybe
he might
be on here
using
this train, it's just
he won't return my calls …"

I blink back

"No, I haven't seen him
but if I do I'll point him
in the direction of your face."
After watching the vacant seats
fail to manifest Jeremy Corbyn
I decide to give up my search

Who am I anyway?

Just a lowly pagan in a black tie
coming back from a funeral

What would I do if I actually saw him on the train?
The same thing I did with Phil Jupitus at Jersey Zoo?

Point and say his name

"You're Phil Jupitus."
"You're Jeremy Corbyn."

I imagine he would say
more than Phil Jupitus

maybe he'd point back
and say
"Hey, aren't you that pagan
wearing a black tie, coming back from a funeral?"

I'd probably stare
a fish in a frying pan
and somehow tumble out

"Tony Blair's face is over there and
he wants a word with you."

Apocalypse
from Gebo, 2021

Drawn curtains
fasten their threads together
never to open again

the pattern does not complete
if not aligned

each chink or fold leaning into the other

Sun's eyes flutter
to brighten the roads
 better than a lick of paint
 better than licking a battery
these jolts will restart the traffic
if only they can navigate
the pot holes and speed bumps
via alternate routes

This must be what summer feels like

And great star, named and unnamed
capturing gaze
yet the cornea do not burn
like they told every froglet
instilled in the pond

distilled in the factories

live it — eat it — pray it — believe it
(you better not believe it)

this scorching sun
sitting in the sky's thoughts
staring down, near enough
to give life to a clump of rock

this sun, inventing time
by parking its arse-cheeks
on the ground
split pantyhose
generate a shadow
around revealed flesh

Seasons of comfort are in session

Goldilocks declares
on the street corners of
The Republic of Poetry — how
it is just right
The shy trees are no more — they
yell jokes from a cannibalistic book
made of their skin
each punchline lands an honest mark
on the face

Somewhere, a statue of a lion whimpers
with its thorn-laced paw
soothed by the tender talons
of a bird of prey — pluck the stick
fuck the splinters
pluck the crone from the maiden's head
as winds
tighten, and tease your throat

Twin bridges
slumped on the River Tamar
filled with silent excuses
to bolt their cables
into a patch of concrete
suspend disbelief
that the inanimate can pass for being human
tread with caution
for a high volume of gendered vehicles
pass this way
hands from the river

claw onto the bank
with Mother Tenacity's affirming grip

the body of Babylon
scooped up in a length of ribbon
dried in a bath towel
kissed on the forehead and sung to sleep

'my bonny lies over a notion…'

where fresh bed sheets
touch static against spines
a taste of seasonal freedom
cruel as the taste of Midsummer Day's goodnight

sleep tight, for now until the turning

Distant suns
replace the glow of proximity
blinking messages through the blackness
into Morpheus's shorthand
typed into dark wanderings
which countdown
to a wake that breaks the mourning

seductive dreams coloured in crayon
until heat melts the wax
sends a hard vibration
through mortal pages
punctuated by prophecy — the end of all days

sat apart
blurry are the smiles
this is the mask
that hides the face
of the spectre of things to be sung
O GREAT REVELATION!

John the Apostle
John the Beatle
Yer Blues blasts loud into the ear

a meeting is scheduled
in the living rooms
of each depredated domicile
dissemination
will dictate the insemination of The Saviour
or the dragon that fell from a city in the clouds

and then silence

And then more silence

The voiceless assemble
in under an hour — rapid response
this is it folks
the moment

THE END OF ALL DAYS HAS COME!

Bled realities flatline — leylines narrow
every channel dried-up and void

The freaks shall inherit the Sun

Demand it ends its exercise routine
 no-more will it rise to offer high-fives
 to drifting angelic forms
 no-more will it be eaten by the groves
 in their grooves as they spin
The Sun pricks its finger

and sleeps one thousand years
cries a thousand more tears
which
evaporate every millisecond
on the burning surface of corruption

Floods eventually consume soils
a sphere sits on the shoulder of a giant
as it trudges through
fresh formed swamps

the pebble stones of the pavement
beat
with a time-signature of 4/4
with lots of ghost notes scattered

Hovering on the edge of their seats
the gods look down
chortle and choke

it is hard to swallow

what remains is a wasteland

And the only hope of ascension
lies in the footnotes of an unwritten poem

a poem worth dying for.

Do You Look at the Moon When I Look at the Moon?
from Gebo, 2021

A slave to the incandescent eye of fate
cast over my body
examining each line to draw conclusions
that the grandeur of a gilded heart
can be dwarfed by existential silence

penetrates every droplet of the soaked clouds
star-walking choirs pool and chorus
their hymn books written in Hebrew
when none of them read Hebrew

Every page stuck to the one before it
turning a corner in the story
forces the slab of words
to crush and press weak fingers

error is, error is marginal
intent unknown
a country waiting to be discovered
when nobody wants it discovered

Remain distant, let your mewling echo
into a stiff chamber of rib bones
wrapping around a diamond
rought, cut from the flesh of a grounded angel

fallen from the side of the divine, fallen

Do you look at The Moon when I look at The Moon?

I Am Why Your Ghost No Longer Speaks
from Gebo, 2021

Your ghost walks by my side
chills iron bars to keep me waking

we navigate the paving slab's follicles
where trees protrude
and clutter The Gray Man's face with green

wise to the woes of Orpheus
the pallid words of his poem

we do not turn; will not turn

cut a finger off to make a compass
whittle down the failed flesh
let it spin, let it spin

This is the street where bombs fell
in perfect iambic pentameter
da DUM da DUM da DUM da DUM da DUM

I am coarse like shrapnel
lodged in the sod

I am why the trees wish to escape
abnormal invading presence

I am why your ghost no longer speaks

staves of an unfinished song tied in knots
syncopated rhythms and a cosmic reunion

Take comfort in faith
as a companion
not in an unmade godhead
but in the all-seeing eye
holy ward — I am waiting

until swallowed by the sallow tears
of the heavens
hand in hand with a deadened dream

Yes, But He Lives in the Philippines
forthcoming in, I Have Eaten the Dead for Breakfast

She said,
"And Bob's your uncle!"
and I replied (as always)
"Yes, but he lives in the Philippines."

And when
the penny dropped down
they said, "and Bob's your uncle!"

"Yes, but he lives in the Philippines." I said

Bob's dead now. So, when they say
"And Bob's your uncle!" and I reply
I add

"Though he is dead now."

I can still remember Bob's body
sliding out the boot of the car
folded neatly in an envelope

He looked like my dad so much
or my dad looks like him I guess
I only met him once
but still, I say "Yes, but he lives in the Philippines."
even now
even though he is dead now

Bob Monkhouse is dead
Bob Marley — dead
Bob Fosee — dead
Bob Hoskins — dead
Bob Hope — dead
Bob Weir — The Grateful Dead, not dead

Matt's Uncle Bob
(who lives in Arizona not the Philippines)
isn't dead

Spencer thinks his dad's brother
was called Bob or Bobby
he is dead

Andrew doesn't have an Uncle Bob
living, dead, or never been alive

All the dinosaurs are dead

Deadweight
Deadbeats
Drop dead gorgeous
dead by The Poets
dead dodos
dead as mutton
brown bread
dead white male
dead dog's eyes
the king is dead, long live the king
kicking dead whales down the beach

Domestos kills all known germs — dead!

They call Domestos, Domex
in the Philippines

you don't need to use multiple cleaners
it works on kitchen surfaces
and floors and bathroom sinks

just spray
quick spray
squirt it and…

Bob's your uncle.

There's That Bridge I Said I Would Cross
forthcoming in, I Have Eaten the Dead for Breakfast

There's that bridge I said I would cross

despite the fear of heights
eating my bones

despite not wearing the right
footwear or socks

In Wuppertal — Germany
rests a Lego bridge
and you can yell Fuck!
when you cross it
and tread on the plastic spines

The Elastic Perspective
in The Netherlands
leads absolutely nowhere
which is where
many of us would like to tread

or there is the Einstein-Rosen bridge
with its compressed matter
temporal heartburn
spacial reflux
and lack of predictability

or there is that bridge I said I would cross
when I came to it

Gargantuan
forthcoming in, I Have Eaten the Dead for Breakfast

I heard the snapping of spines — the seals once fused
to prop up the acropolis of greater man's marvel

those that fuelled the veins and arteries of civilisation
filled them with liquid mercury to measure their fever
they who shunned the masters and missionaries
and placed marbles in their pockets to sink deeper

who rebelled against a notion of notoriety in-exchange for
compromising their natural complexion and in their turn —
gained fucking notoriety

broke their bellies by ingesting the soup of chaos and
holding it in, bound in skin and raw meat, assimilated
through a supplement regiment of zoots and the fruits of
bass heavy rack

they who roamed reason and found it deserted — roasted
by the midday sun and the anarchy of the moon until they
were caught in the snatch of wild beasts

their sugar-coated growls expelled into hollow caves
sneaking past the guards of decency — disguised as an
echo

prophecy is a bomb

detonates amnesia as alchemy to transmute ethos
human sacrifice in order to achieve humanity

THE SELF erupts into ironic glints of problematic wiles
which indulge THE SELF to liberate THE SELF

— fucked into existence
— fucked by existence
— fucked

out of their souls, and their minds, and their bodies, and
their homes, left to breathe the streets of the imagination
and there conjuring the conjectures of animated corpses
— enough to garner nods and murmurs from the widows of
promise, widowed by apathy, lethargy, leaving no room
for repartee to be processed and understood
save the second-hand photos from the charity shop - keep
them alive on an ofrenda made of offensive heresy

a beauty pageant won by misnomer

this dystopia is autobiographical
and these are indeed dystopian times

leaves them remanded yet they remain receptive
to the ruminations of the past, resign themselves to be the
minstrels of madness who will testify in an open court of
sons and daughters, defend the unseen and unborn

it is not permissible
as so often we are lead to believe

the truth?

Six o'clock is too late for coffee but not to fuck
(keep it in your holster, cowboy)

God loves a cappuccino — takes a stroll down the road
skips along slabs, buffed and polished with indifference

catches the scent of bakers shaping loaves for the Early
Morning rise, loaves made from white-bred lies and
banker's cocaine — bread so foul even the ducks won't
chow it down

ducks preferring their own vomit
from fear of digestive disorders
commonly associated with
an unhealthy diet of unpleasantness

spies the impossible people lost between the margins of
the page, ponders over cancel culture and how they would
have killed Plath or Ginsberg had they not already been
killed by curiosity
spots bags of hope dumped outside food banks — signs
reading "feed your babes on dead butterflies" for nothing
flies in the gravity of this situation

shamanic burning sessions erupt in the bars, flaming
spirits rupture reality — working hard for the weekend

banshees wailing as they win or lose at cards
— this is where they fight — this is where they stab — and fuck

this is where they smoke chokey, cover the commotion of
the locomotive bodies as they pump their skunk-dust into
the air

practice smiling
isometric exercises are devalued by the lies of the skulless
(were we jellyfish we'd swim)

sorries airing worries, dried and crinkled but smelling
damp, taken in as the night begins to cough

dropped copies of spiritual manifestos left bereft on park
benches — there to keep slats warm for the unhomed
swarms who will flock and forage come twilight's heavy-
tongued kiss

incurable of their dishonesty – the warlords declare law

take to your fridges – HIDE! Know your own mind enough
to recognise the birthday cake orbiting in the corner

you will outsmart any goldfish
if you keep your head out of the bowl

scoff at inequality
— the great denial
— the one being greater than ten, or twenty
this is tardigrades crushed into the lunar surface
choking on Selene's skin flakes

being promised a glimpse
of brioche from the breakfast table
in a penthouse apartment in New York Shitty

this is gargantuan

because you are gone
and you get it
and you do it and live it

angriness comes endowed with a ten inch cock
to fuck some sense into us

monged by pandemonium, we run our tongues along the
ground, catch gravel in the grooves, chew the stones and
spit into the pit of reason and revolution

THEY ARE ONE IN THE SAME – can't you tell?

We're our betters
— your BBC is on its knees — mouth open
— your NHS trafficked away
— your carbonated dreams kept in the can

dreams pissed on by the rats and mice that live in palaces
but frequent common places to vent their arrogance in
streams

this is the only live stream you need
for your eyes alone

Artemis and Apollo
and the Theory of the Sun

Apollo and Aphrodite
asking for The Moon

see what can happen when you take the napkin off your
lap, wipe the blood from your mouth and ask to see the
menu

claim back some self-respect — know the worth of two
pennies — lift your chin, and your hips, and LIVE

before the great minds succumb to the drummed in
affirmations expelled daily and programmed in through
throwaway phrasing

eat books
read people

open your minds to the sound of your universe
vibrate
defy physics like a fat, little bumble-bee
and ascend rightly
into the realms
reserved for higher thinking

tip the tables over like cows, let the cows loose from the
supermarkets, buy your groceries from Mutley's temples
and stockpile enough to see you through this harsh cunt of
a winter

because the summer rains will come to fill your cup
 tell the spinners to shut their fucking noise
sip your cold coffee
and write yourself
a goddamn poem

for we —
We are dirt We are cringe
We are legion We are knots
We are teeth We are sighs
We are bought and weighed

We are into We are out of
We are deficit of fucks
We are the babes and boom
We are acid jazz We are pop

We are retracted We are synth
We are hybrids of time and space
We are leviathans We are kids

We are the dynamos and drums
We are fucking hilarious
We are wrapped up We are under
We are thumbs and thimbles

We are wooden sticks to rub
We are lycra We are velcro
We are limping as we run wild
We are whimpers in the womb

We are greater than our parts
We are in search of the whole
We are gifted starlings on string
We are receipts for travel

We are shampoos and soaps
We are canvas We are corporeal
We are creeps We are special
We are ash and its roar

We are more than our membership
We are lightning fast and furious
We are an expulsion of dark matter
We are The Big Bang or Big Bopper
We are the itch and the rains
We are tattoos on the skins of trees
We are rationed We are irrational
We are walkers We are wanderers

JAMES BRIDGWATER

TRUTH

The Church

Walls of stone, so cold and uninviting,
I see no signs of love, divine and never quitting.
Windows with stained glass, do not attract great hoards,
No hint of honour or respect, for what should be the Lord's.
But crumbling old church buildings are not where you'd best look,
Just simply read the news, contained in God's good book.

Cathedral, synod, and such words, our Saviour never used.
The word religion, is there one, so utterly abused.
The churches which achieve the most are those we know the least,
In countries where it hurts to look, Christianity seems ceased.
But underground the faith keeps on, and martyrs fight for truth,
Lost their families by now, the kids must risk their youth.

God's servants here are different in the material West,
It's more about having a good Sunday best.
And reducing the contact, with societies misfits,
From the Bible pick the nice and easy bits.
Rapists, drug-users, homosexuals, drunkards on the floor.
With faith, they'll beat a millionaire through the heavenly door.

Emotions are hard work

I've seen and heard The Scream,
It's not my fault, I'm not to blame.
I wish I'd been taught about emotions.
Instead of Chemistry, Physics and Biology
I'd have done a course in Emotional Management,
If it had been an option.

My Mum died in front of me, when I was 5 years old.
Alone in boarding school, and then a young offenders place.

I played with drugs and emotions
For a year in Manchester,
But then depression hit me
And I tried to kill myself.

I wish I'd an A' level or two
In qualifications like Love and Hate
I know a guy with those tattooed on his knuckles.

A Masters in Sadness would help me deal with things,
But I'd rather have a Doctorate in Applied Happiness.
But experiences are a help to deal with new events.
Transactional Analysis and Therapy,
Life Coaching and determined grit.
Have got me where I am.
I enjoy my life these days, and I'm glad I'm who I am.

Wyndham Street West

Stonehouse is a great place to live,
The Catholic cathedral between me and town.
Support for the aged decaying nuns they give.
In their residential home enduring lockdown.

St. Peter's High church, C of E resides in Wyndham Square,
It's converted convent and school have become flats now.
Between the two churches Hollywood Terrace thoroughfare
A European style walkway paved, and secure trees does endow.

At times each institution rings their bells, for a service or the hour.
Yet like many Christian denominations they are not together,
Despite what they'd gain if they united to share hardship and power.
Nearby Stoke Damerel church Protestants do spiritually endeavour;

It has been thus for centuries as it's an ancient Plymouth site.
Easter should be a time for Christians to join together,
But Covid-19 virus ruined that, leaving an uncertain plight.
2020 Easter I'll recall alone in lovely weather.

Alphabet Poem

A is a single thing,
B is an insect,
C sounds like the big wide ocean.
D is the Jamaican definitive article, as in 'Where is D joint?'
E is the drug of the 90s raves.
F is the short polite way to swear.
G the women's' secret spot.
H's often get dropped at the start of words.
I is me not you.
J is the single letter for a spliff,
K a special cereal.
L is a Roman 50 while
M is their 1000.
N a negative letter.
O an exclamation of surprise.
P is the little green ball in a pod.
Q, what we British don't like to do.
R ahead of 1st half of Bible acronym is what many people think God is.
S pluralises many things.
T the British favourite drink from India and China.
U the sound of the 2nd person
V equates to victory and also number 5.
W ahead of Mrs chicken ask the time of question.
X marks a spot.
Y the letter at the end of the questioning word it is off.
Z completes the collection of 26 symbols which can portray anything.

Truth

Truth should be told as testimony,
The whole and nothing but.
Testimony comes from testicles
And that's a load of balls.

Balls are spherical, that's true
But the world really does seem flat.
People don't fall off the edge
Despite they used to fear that.

Transformation, we need in this nation.
This country is in a state, the state is in a mess.
The government can't run the place
Departments run to rack and ruin.

The N.H.S. is falling down and breaking at the seams.
The same applies to prison staff.
And all the services we need.
Foodbanks and homeless shelters are everywhere.

Opposites Attract

I'm intellectual, you are emotional.
You know families, I do not.
You are practical, I am spiritual.
You have few friends, I've a lot

I am weak, you are strong.
I use few words, you use a lot.
My time with a partner's short, yours is long.
You like things in order, I do not.

I am serious, you play games.
I'm tight with money, you are not.
You are Victoria, I am James.
I hope you like me, I like you a lot.

I eat every day and I like to cook.
You enjoy American TV and I don't.
You like to make things, I want to write a book.
You may give up on me but I hope you won't.

What is Love?

Love is a four letter word.
Love is a rearranged vole.
Love is seven points at Scrabble.
Love is one of the great poetry themes. Love is a rhyme of dove.
Love is the most valuable, priceless gift.
Love is a non-concrete noun.
Love is the difference between humans and animals.
Love is what needs to be the prefix of Craft to name a great Gothic
    writer.
Love is a couple of vowels and a couple of consonants.
Love is the root of all evil when applied to money.
Love is a whitewash at tennis.
Love is a verb, both transitive and intransitive.
Love is the drug according to Roxy Music.
Love is the antonym of hate.
Love is one hand of tattooed knuckles.
Love is what drives me to stand up here in front of you and read a
    piece of verse.
Love is like the measles, something we all have to go through,
    according to Jerome K. Jerome.
Love is such a mystery, I cannot find it out.
Love is the food for music.
Love is the largest source of quotes in the Oxford Dictionary of
    Quotations.
Love is the greatest of faith, hope and love. Love is love.

Father

Shoulders strong for burden bearing,
They've had their fair share and more too.
Emotional and physical,
He takes my mishaps in his stride.

But solid shoulders which take so much
Are yet so soft when cried upon.
Like pillows made from silk wrapped lace,
A bear hug from the endless well of love.

The question is, when Dad's not there?
For some people he never was,
Or wasn't what he should have been.
Violence. Drink. I could but need not list some more.

For them of course there's Father God,
The strongest shoulders of the lot.
Never too busy to hear you out,
He heads the best family I know.

Prayer

Prayer takes on another
character when one is
desperate. It's an energy,
the sudden realisation that
you are very justified
to beseech literal God,
who made you, and
is ultimately responsible.
The vegetative essence
animates dirt into
electric meat, which cannot
leave off imagining
new futures, even while
running from
monsters. The meat
asks God's wheel
to turn, which it
invariably does. What
every clock must
measure is answered
prayers.

I have news

I have news that
is so truly splendid
that it sets dragonflies
to racing:
in the feathered crowd,
I found the one particular
angel that swops deaths.
Bedizened with charms
and wishes, wrought in
every matter we use
to make words manifest:
the sinews of rats, platinum
chain, cobweb, spun
diamond. All saying, take
me instead. And she will!
All those thousands of
nopeopes and sorryorries,
I forgot what yes sounds
like. In this case, a form,
vellum and a script that
looks drawn by an art nouveau
elf. I have filled it out
and I have a date, Thursday!
I am so excited you
have no idea. I will die owing
poems to a lot of people,
and have given the list,
and the poems,
to this kind angel. They will
inhere to the
dreams of them I
swop with, whether it
is a little baby or
a gaffer or another

chased prey. You will
have to appeal to them
to settle my accounts,
for I have finally discovered
the flavour of mercy

Dice

Pick the dice you want to roll.
Don't toss any accidental
out the window, down a hole.
Honestly, it drives me mental
keeping track of elves and mice.
In school, they said it was simple—
get the orange, or the coal.
Pick the dice you want to roll.

Comets

What the comets know,
they keep.
Bending their arcs as they sleep,
passing by once a year.
Shine brightly and go,
knowing we note
passage of each shining mote,
forgetting to ask
anything. Patiently draw
each, in its time and its fall.
In blinks, watching faces,
running their rails,
tugging the faintest of traces
of those they passed,
this time, the next one, the last.

The Poems Will Come Back

The poems will
come back.
Solemnly, I swear
they are still there,
waiting.
Roots twine round
the gratings,
flourish or fail,
clog with leaves
and little balls
of hail,
stop rain.
In the flood,
poems hide
amidst frogspawn
and bright yellow snails.
When storm passes
and light fills
the crystalline drip,
the butterflies sip.
I write these
words, not long
for this world.
Green leaf, still
tightly furled,
dead, snapped
by the wind.
Lost before start.
But poems, they
grow in the heart
of the tree,
creosote-black—
and come back.

The Angerbird

The angerbird
spawns in the
gizzards of seagulls
and the eggs
are vomited into
the sea, cared for
by mermaids in
their royal gardens,
and then, they hatch
full-fledged, and
settle on the desks
of the forgetters
and stabbers of
hideous women. If
there is a strange
artifact on the video
of the evening news,
it is likely an
angerbird, staring
into the eye of
a fearfuller of we
trash-women. She waits,
is their call. She waits.

I cannot tell you yet

I cannot tell you
yet, but I can enter
the vestibule
to the anteroom
of telling you,
dust the mustard
yellow cushions,
polish the lacquered
screen. A reflection
of a reflection
might tell you
that I saw a post
of a grey cat
who's father
let him outside
before walking
off the precipice.
Our consciousness
crosses the bridges
between universes.
I have here a
ticket made of
gold, to a train
that reaches
a flower-filled station,
and in the little
house, my brother
opened the window
and his grey
cat leapt out,
and was trapped
weeks later, by
a weeping friend
who took him home.

In the town surrounding
that little station,
where the sun is
very slightly redder,
there is a
grey cat with
baleful yellow eyes
cocking his head
at the ghostly sound
of the creak of a
hinge, a door
that will never open
again.

Morrison's Automatic Tills

Morrison's automatic tills
tell you: surprising item
in the bagging area.
I imagine a woman with a way
with words, like me,
came up with the idea
to call it surprising, not
unexpected. Can a robot
be surprised? Can it
expect? It is we
who are surprised,
not knowing which
flat expanse of metal
is the bagging area.
School will teach
our children to think
like robots, to pass
through swiftly,
to breathe once
they get back to the car.

LYN DOUGLASS

THE BOWLING GREEN

Jeffrey is the head coach of Lemington Bowling Green. His bulbous form stands at the far side of the short grass.

"Hurry up. Roll it to me," he bellows.

I deeply inhale, swing my arm up, and hurl. The bowl twists through the air and thuds to the ground a metre away. As I raise my head I watch the Hitler-like figure, moustache in tow, striding up the green. He stops short of my nose. Eyeball to eyeball, his shiny red face ogles. Captain Jeffery Snodgrass's false teeth rattle. As he fumes, his body seems to expand. I shiver. Will this be my first and last experience of bowling?

My partner, Steve, persuades me to come to club night, where new and experienced players mingle together. Here the format of the game is explained. The little yellow ball is called a Jack. The team comprises of four players. The lead's job is to draw the wood (bowl) close to the Jack. Number two likewise. The role of number three is to safeguard the bowls or fire (whack it) to rid the opposition. The player also measures the wood to establish which is nearest to the Jack. Skip instructs the rest of the team and must succeed if they screw up

I sign up to friendly games but soon discover that my inexperience and slowness is causing irritation to the team. My wood looks like it's auditioning for Tchaikovsky's dying swan. On the bench sits Michael, a retired bowler, wrapped in a thick anorak, although the sun is hot. The swinging up continues. Another player asks why I'm performing the shot-put.

There are many county matches played on the green. With supremacy, the veteran bowlers, dressed in white tailored trousers and starched shirts, stroll on. In awe, the novices watch the experts roll their woods an inch from the Jack. I hide in the shadows, away from the jocularity of the others, dreading the teasing. Michael watches. Although he sees me as a lost cause, he's eager to help. After a few months of gentle supervision, I manage to keep the bowl on the correct rink.

"I think I'm a bit better, Mike. It's been difficult using the wrong hand."

"What do you mean?"

"I'm left-handed. I didn't want to be different, so I used my right like everyone else."

Mike, shaking his head, moves back to the bench.

I walk home with Steve who's rattling on about his team's victory. He was the one that suggested bowling could be a gentle hobby for us. Little did I know that these elderly pensioners are deadly competitive and bitterly venomous. At times, it seems impossible to decipher the difference between them and disruptive children, deliberately barging into each other on the green. Verbal and a few physicals frequently occur.

"You coughed just as I was bowling."

The men's league matches are played at the weekends. I watch a player bend to measure the wood when the opposition kicks it out of the way. It results in a blast of swearing. The culprit is pushed over. Legs creaking, he pulls himself up and marches off with two fingers in the air.

Each member pays a yearly affiliation fee. A democratic club, I think. but soon realise that embedded in this activity is a small hierarchy. One day I spy a few of the committee sat in the Italian café and eavesdrop.

"Did you see Brian? He was wearing a white cap with '*I love Looe*' printed on the side. England Bowls would never allow that." They begin whispering. I strain to hear. "And we've got to sort that Bert out. Don't think he's had a wash, let alone bath, for weeks."

*

I crouch down, bowl in my hand, when the captain hisses in my ear that I mustn't wear black knickers as they can be seen through white trousers. I let out a cackle.

Captain Marjorie frowns. "Ten years ago, we had an exceptionally large lady. Must have been twenty stone. Well," she clears her throat, "when she bent down, we could see she was wearing a purple G-string … Yes, a sight never to be forgotten. Please adhere to the regulations."

At the AGM meeting discussions centre on refreshments. "Why can't the men have cheese crackers?" shouts Henry. "Some of us don't like custard creams. Who's in charge?" After twenty minutes of shouting, the floor decides the biscuits remain.

Under Health and Safety, the Secretary reads out a letter from one of the visiting clubs. *"It has come to our attention that one of our members endured extreme shock and mental distress. Mrs Andress, an eighty-year-old lady, found herself locked in your Pavilion on July 17th. She hadn't realised how late it was and most of the women had left including the key holder. After screaming for more than thirty minutes, someone alerted the police. The only way of freeing the poor woman was to pull her through a small window. Fortunately, Mrs Andress is a slight woman so was able to be released."* A titter breezes around the room.

Under 'Any Other Business,' several members voice the issue of women wearing shorts.

"Put your hand up and wait until I say you can speak," cries the Secretary. "And keep it brief."

"That's the problem, the briefness," shouts Bert. "I should not have to look at all this flesh when I am measuring the woods. At my age, I don't want a coronary."

A woman next to me chuckles that they should bring up the subject of flatulence and points to a member. "She bent down and let out a noise like a squeaking balloon. Blamed it on chickpeas."

With Mike's help, I warily sign up to the league playing with other Cornish clubs. At the beginning of the match each competitor shakes the rival's hand with the intent of injuring her, saying "Have a good game." Once the skip became so enraged by one of her players, she threw her hat to the ground. After each end, the terrified woman walked on the edge of the green for fear of her life.

I learn quickly never, ever ask, "How are you?" What follows is a pyramid of human body defects. The most common are knee and hip disorders followed by diabetes and hypertension. Frequently septuagenarians trip and fall on the green. Shocked, I watched at bowlers walking around wailing bodies.

"Got to think of my health. Could do my back in trying to pull him up."

Invariably an ambulance is called, hauling the patient into the back and off to hospital. But after a few days the invalid is soon out playing.

Weather plays a large part in bowling. Organisers of the games have the task of deciding whether the match should go ahead. There are days when rain and wind interfere with the player's ability. The captain's position is to consult with the greenkeeper as to whether the ground is too sodden. Frequently she will okay the play, desperate for matches not to be cancelled. I had my first experience of these conditions, descending the slippery steps to the green. Dressed in white waterproof outfits, our heads covered with hoods, reminded me of twenty odd people looking like a cluster of condoms.

I placed my bowls on the green and tried wiping the mist from my lens, but the smears made it worse. Like a penguin losing its way I eventually settled on the mat and rolled the wood. It skidded into another rink. The opposition took her turn. Drips of water slid from her hood, onto nose and rolled down her neck. She bowled and slid off the mat in the direction of the wood. Her team lifted the crumpled woman up and patted her back for trying. The third player found her legs splayed like a dog on ice. I couldn't stop myself grinning but this time it was serious, and paramedics were called. Only Jean can pitch her wood onto the green. But then, as another woman told me, she has arms like a gorilla.

It's time for tea and biscuits. The captain rings the bell demanding attention. "I'm afraid we're not going out again. I have been told that Silvia might have fractured her hip and it is too dangerous to continue. Also, Mary has informed me she has wet knickers and bra."

The women change out of their wet gear, their hair soaked and mascara running down cheeks. A few are still outside gathering saturated equipment. Before long, the home team get themselves organized, and help laying out crockery and bringing in tea pots. It's time to sit down, to warm up with the brew and bring out the custard creams. Daisy needs to be watched. She will try and shove as many biscuits in her mouth as she can, interfering with the ratio of one and a half biscuits.

Covid had closed the green for two years. Now, it's the start of a new season. Mike has come out of retirement, my partner in the mixed pairs. Our opponents are Jeffery Snodgrass, red faced as ever and Captain Marjorie. I win the toss and begin. My bowl sits sweetly on the Jack.

"Well done," shouts Mike.

Marjorie heaves, then groans. She has rolled with the wrong bias and her wood flies in the opposite direction.

Snodgrass screams. "Stupid woman!"

Bowlers congregate by the Pavilion. My excellent delivery continues, four woods on the Jack. Snodgrass is not pleased. He marches to the mat, his shoulders rocking back and forth. Mike rolls the first of his woods and draws to an inch of the Jack. Jeffery must fire and remove our bowls. He takes aim but narrowly misses. He tries again and again. Jefferey has a tantrum, jumping up and down.

The crowd cheers. Marjorie sneers. Her ill fortune continues and Snodgrass's rage swells. The more he explodes, the more incompetent Marjorie plays. We win 18/0 and stroll off the green to loud merriment.

Thank goodness Mike saw a tiny piece of ability in that hopeless novice years ago.

The queue extends along the car park. People two metres apart. It reminds Sally of images from The Second World War. Jews waiting to board the death trains. The child skips away from her mother's side.

"Go away."

Stevie knows it's her other mummy speaking. A grey pebble face.

"Don't worry, Mum. I'll make it better." Two people come out of the supermarket. Now it's their turn. "Can I have a chocolate cake?"

Sally feels paralysed. Aisles shrinking. Voices. "Can't remember what …"

"Lollies, pizza, lemonade … and cake." All food that Stevie desires.

The child's arms are too short. "You get it." Stevie pulls her mother to the freezer. Squeals, as items fling into the trolley. "You push it." Sally is rigid. "I'll do it, Mum."

The contraption swings, crashing into a shopper.

"Discipline that brat of yours and keep your distance. Can't you see that I'm vulnerable?"

Stevie bites her lip, waiting for a reaction.

"Piss off," Sally retorts, holding up two fingers with a frozen stare. They reach the check-out. Excitedly, Stevie heaves items towards the counter. Most fall to the floor.

"You should be in charge. Not leaving her to go riot," says an irritable cashier. "That will be thirty pounds and twenty pence."

Sally searches her bag. Fingers tingle. The purse drops to the floor.

"I'll get it, Mummy. Don't worry."

"Only got ten pounds."

They leave with lollies, pizza, and a large chocolate cake. Hot humid air presses down. Sally's clockwork body marches the trolley towards the beach. Stevie runs. Little legs trying to keep up with her mother. She pants, holding the package to her chest. "Mummy, are we having a picnic?"

Sally crumples to the sand. Hands cradling head.

Stevie clambers into the trolley, slinging foodstuffs to the ground. Tearing open the cardboard box, she sinks her teeth into the gluey sponge. "Mum, have some … Want to go for a wee."

The beach is desolate. Stevie runs towards the water, drops her knickers, and piddles. Her mother mumbles to those people that Stevie can't see. Sometimes that mummy can't see her. Stevie puts a shell to her ear. Sounds of gushing, hushing.

Sally jabs her face. "Leave me alone," she screams.

Stevie dances towards Sally. "Yes, leave my Mummy alone. Chase you away. Run, run." She circles, creating ripples in the sand. Stevie trips over Sally's handbag. The contents spill. "Oh dear." A silver sheet glints. Stevie thrusts the medication to Sally's mouth. "Take Mummy's sweeties."

The child builds a sandcastle while Sally sleeps. The thawed lollies bleed patterns in the sand. Sun dissolves into the sea. The tide surges forward, sloshing the trolley's wheels.

Salt-water wakes Sally. Thrusting up her wet body, she groggily looks around. "Stevie, where are you?"

Her daughter's small figure is splashing, oblivious to the sea heaving. The swell is approaching.

"Stevie," she yells. "I'm coming. Don't worry. Mummy will make it better."

Diane pulls out the decomposing leaves of the lilies, their slumped heads wilting, and lays them in the newspaper. The church is dark, foreboding. She is alone and reminisces.

"I vowed to obey his every wish at the marriage ceremony. Twenty-five years of putting up with crap."

What was that about? Scrubbing his dirty underpants, putting up with his drinking bouts, his hands up some poor cow's skirt. And all that time I smiled sweetly to the world, glamoured up at the dinner parties and endured the sweaty sickening sex. Was this what they called making love?

My friend said it's the same for all of us and I've got to try and make the best of it.

He planned four children. I didn't want any, but along came Julian, and Rose three years later. Then I found the pill. Huh.

Not once did I share my moans at the W.I. Or the meals on wheels. Or the community library. Just smiled sweetly.

Julian played football. It was him who got the flashy bike, the latest mobile and trainers.

It was a different story for my Rose. "Help your mother in the kitchen and tidy your room," he bellowed

I tried to fight her corner, but he held the purse strings. "It's a man's world," he sniggered. But as my little girl grew, she became single-minded. She knew what she wanted. Rose's confidence flourished and ambitions soared. My daughter didn't take shit from anyone and graduated with a first-class degree. A few years later, she started a successful interior design enterprise on the internet.

It was about this time that the menopause started. I heard stories about hot flushes, mood swings, dry vaginas and going off sex. My red-faced friends craved for open windows, sweat dripping from their armpits, desperate for icy lollies. But it didn't happen to me. My high oestrogen levels declined, I felt normal, neurosis free. The chrysalis opened.

One day, I looked at my husband. The balding creature, belly protruding, yellowing teeth decaying. A plonker! That time, when he demanded, I walked away. One day he rushed forward to slap me. Imagining a cleaver in my hand, I punched him in the face. And again.

Then I left. He couldn't bully me now. Rose said that us women didn't have to fit into a man's culture. She found me a nice flat in the Italian quarter. I resumed my career in publishing and Rose created a website. Doing well, thank you.

I started thinking of all the bastards that had hurt me. They didn't call it sexual harassment back then. Smacking bottoms, touching breasts was just fun and trapping you in the loo! Well, you asked for it. Time to dish out punishments.

My plan was to shatter their façades. Leave them naked to the world. Flesh stripped. Their skulls floating in their own pollution. Facebook, Twitter, emails. I sent them all. Anonymous of course.

Other women tweeted. Abused, ashamed victims. The newspapers ran with it. I watched these men fall apart as investigations began. I laughed when the media interviewed politicians, business tycoons, policemen, royalty, floundering, spitting out lies. Caught in their own shit, with their trousers down.

Diana fills the vases with clean water and orange dahlias, their shiny green leaves glistening.

"These days I don't have to smile sweetly, but I do."

BINGO NIGHT

It is ten past six on a Friday evening. Bill, armed with boxes and carrier bags, kicks open the door and walks towards the bottom of the hall. He places the coloured dabs and bingo books the left side of the stage. A hazy silence collects in the large space. Bill's heavy breathing is his only companion. Slinging his coat over a chair, Bill shoves three long tables together. Shaky arthritic fingers place a cash box with the rest of the items, including the raffle prizes, onto the middle bench. Teabags, (people moan if they're not included), meat vouchers, a bottle of wine and the fruit basket, nobody wants. His emaciated body push four chairs towards each of the twelve small tables. Bill looks up and sighs. A single balloon from the Christmas party six months ago, hangs from the ceiling. He sniffs, remembering his deceased wife and the fun they had.

Bill has managed Bingo for fifteen years. It's his baby. Numbers have dropped, but on a good night forty punters could arrive. He waits for his two volunteers, but first to arrive is Mavis, an elderly woman and one of Bill's most loved customers. She sits in the same seat, alone. A few people have tried to occupy this place but have met with Mavis's wrath. Before retiring she was a matron, some say a dictator, in the NHS. Tells Bill she never had any problems with the patients, only the consultants.

Bill shouts over to the tiny bird-like figure. "Had a good week, Mavis?"

"Fine dear. The children came over Sunday for my birthday. They do try, but the presents! Not to my liking." She makes a face.

Bill chuckles and continues his chores. Next to enter is Sally, who helps sell the bingo books. Widowed ten years ago, her downcast face seems fixed, circulating an air of doom into the room.

The other assistant, Vera, saunters down the hall. Her ruddy brown face beaming. She rubs her hands together. "Hi gang. Back to awful weather."

"All right for some. Some that's been in Thailand for the last three months," grimaces Mavis.

The hall begins to fill. The crowd from Waitrose sit away from the others, opposed to being contaminated by the Lidl's peasants. Bill, with a loud wheeze, shouts that the tickets are ready. An orderly line forms.

Doris parks her mobility scooter in the foyer and pushes to the front of the queue. "I'm disabled and can't stand for long." Conversation about various diseases and amputations begin. Doris shrinks away.

Tom, Bert, Stan and John have never missed a bingo night. They shuffle to their seats and each position three coloured markers by their boards. John's eyes have deteriorated, but he's adamant there's nothing wrong. He pulls out a magnifying glass.

Richard, a widower, sits on the adjoining table. He pats Bert on the back. The elderly man hisses. "You. Don't touch me!"

Nobody knows why he refuses to speak to Richard, but it's been going on for years. The door swings open and Grace arrives. She is always late, but Bill has already put her tickets to one side. Grace pays with the fifth twenty pound note of the evening. There is no change. All helpers grumble and Bill searches his pockets. With a nervous titter, Grace scoops up her cards and joins the elderly men.

"Put your name on the back of the tickets and you might win a pound," smirks Stan.

He tells Grace this every Bingo night. She nods. Stan is eighty-five and fancies Grace. He pushes his chair close, his hand fondling her knee. Grace does nothing. The attention is welcome. As a seventy-year-old, frivolous touching has long passed her. Grace gazes at another woman, Gloria, whose munching pork scratchings. Her globular cheeks look as if they are about to burst. Yes, Gloria the Gerbil, she thinks.

Bill joins Grace and the elderly four men. He looks under the table, and Stan takes his hand off Grace's knee. The first game is about to start and there is a hushed silence of anticipation. On stage sits the caller, Theo with his microphone and bingo machine. He's dressed in a tight check suit, a gold bow tie strangling his neck.

Theo booms at the scattering of people. "Have you all got your bingo tickets, my lovelies?"

"No," shout two people at the bar. One waits for a glass of water, the other a cup of tea. The Social Club always makes a loss when bingo is on. The barmaid, hair tied into a ponytail, chews gum. The old people annoy her, and she slams the beverage down on the counter. Tea splatters on the man's hand. He screams with pain, pointing at the offender.

The crowd are impatient. 'Hurry up and sit down.'

"Tonight, the line is £4, the house is £9, and the flyer is £40, you lovely people." Theo chuckles. "Life changing money." The machine starts and Theo begins. "Two fat ladies, eighty-eight."

"Can't say that!" pipes up Grace. "That's discrimination."

"Oh, shut up," yells one of the Waitrose women. "Let's get on with the game."

Betty sits sucking eclairs beside her friend, Irene. Her hair is immaculate. Betty tells everyone she attends the hairdressers for a wash and set each week, but Bill knows it's a wig. Betty's voice is like a knife scratching on glass. "Eeeh!" she screams. Bill checks her card and deposits four coins into shrivelled hands.

Theo continues. "Six and nine. Sixty nine, anyway up," he titters.

Grace yells, "Perv." Stan gently strokes her back.

The house is won by The Gerbil, who is now on her second packet of pork scratchings. Mavis waves Grace over. She whispers. "Only been a member for three months and that woman always wins."

Theo shouts, "Half-time. Get your beers and smoke your fags."

Bill wanders round the hall making sure the people are enjoying themselves.

Stan draws close to Grace. "See Bill flirting with Margaret? He's after someone to go on holiday with. Wife only gone nine months and he's looking for another woman." Stan's flushed face sniggers. "He's got quite a few ladies he's after. See her behind the bar?" Grace turns and looks at a short squat woman serving a customer with a menacing stare. "She said she couldn't go away with him because her estranged husband is likely to move into her house if she goes on holiday."

Grace sniffs. "None of my business or yours, Stan."

A dozen punters wander onto the balcony and light up. Mavis joins Grace who tells her she used to have a full-time job in a mental hospital, as well as being a mother of five children. In a Scottish lilt she retells stories of controlling violent patients and juggling her time with the family. "Honestly, more nutters here than there."

The smokers cough their way back to the hall and bingo resumes. Irene calls after her number has gone. "Sorry love, you shouted too late." Theo is sympathetic. Irene is not pleased and whines to her friend that she did call. A couple sitting at the next table argue that they didn't hear her, and an argument begins.

A brassed off Bill stands up. "Be quiet, you lot, or else we'll terminate the bingo!" There are indignant murmurs, followed by a hush.

Theo resumes. "The last house is the Flyer." Elasticated necks hover over the pink sheet of numbers. Grace's lucky pen is poised. Theo begins. Grace crosses one number and another. She holds her breath.

"Doctor's orders, number nine."

"Yes, yes," shouts Grace, waving her fist in the air.

Poker faced Sally begrudgingly hands over the cash. Theo tells any newcomers to print their names at the back of the tickets. Vera collects them in a bucket and asks one member to pick out three. Each winner receives £1. A grinning Bert takes his coin. The finale is raffle prizes and Gloria wins a box of teabags. Doris snarls. She has won nothing. Bingo is over, and people rush to catch buses. Gloria is engrossed, stuffing more crisps down her throat. Doris seems to have forgotten her disability. She pinches the teabags and streaks out of the hall.

Bill takes a deep breath and begins clearing the tables of used books, sweet wrappers, and soggy tissues. He scratches his beard. Not a bad night, all considered.

HEATHER GRANGE

LA VIE EST BELLE

Belgium at Christmas

I sip coffee behind warm glass,
watch the young Flemish,
the descendants of wool merchants,
turn up their coats against the wind,
eat at McDonalds,
cycle everywhere.
The Big Wheel turns slowly on the square.
'Everybody's younger than me!'
The jutting gables, tall windows,
red and yellow bricks and cobbles say:
'Not as old as us! Not as old as us!'

Menton

A Russian and English church,
Westminister, and Prince de Galles hotels,
history makes a long call.
In the old quarter, rounded arches,
a market, orange bricks,
green shutters keep out the afternoon heat,
orange and lemon trees.
Musicians play on the square.
Italian is spoken here.
At the Trattoria de Mamma,
Salade Nicoise, cockles in olive oil,
Rose ice cream.
'We've come here fifty times,' two diners say,
leaving a good tip
'One hundred, you'll get the tee-shirt!'
the owner replies.
In a world of cotton shirts, flip flops,
short sleeves, children head for the beach,
elderly, well dressed ladies, hurry
through the door of the Community Centre
for the Third Age.

Lavender and Oleander

In an old farmhouse nestling in the hills
amid the oleander and lavender
we spent hot July days by the pool
reading a book or taking a siesta.
Franki and Dave walked around bare foot,
Dave's ankles swelled up.
In the early morning we strolled down in the heat
to buy pastries and bread.
Charles bought a Panama in the market,
a Dirk-Bogarde-in-Venice lookalike.
At nightfall it was pitch black,
the shutters were closed to keep out mosquitoes
but there was always one!
The smells of the lavender bags bring it all back.

Blacksmith's Lane Primary School, 1953

A mystery arithmetic, the teacher antagonistic,
stretching herself on her wedged shoes
and me on the rack in tears.
A bore reciting tables by rote,
Mr. Porter's lessons on geography
and the Canadian Prairies.
A joy Saint David's Day, daffodils in lapels,
being dressed as an angel in the Nativity,
receiving third prize on Prize-Giving Day.
On his visits, instilling fear the policeman Mr. Mills.
A stiff upper lip for Mr. Crouch's limp,
made a prisoner by the Japanese.
In needlework frustration,
pulling a thread through a gingham apron.
Memories of the smells of carrots, new laid linoleum, cloakrooms,
seeing Mr Davies, the Head, and Miss Pomphlett, dignified
pedalling home on their bikes.

276 Wightman Road (1968)

A house beginning to expire
whose first occupants serviced an empire
or joined a gold rush.
When little girls were seen not heard,
an Englishman's bond his word.
Slowly declining from an industrial peak
not surviving stock market crashes
like blasts of air through broken sashes.
'Furnished rooms to let,' bed, wobbly table, armchair.
Notice: 'Gentlemen Please Flush,'
thin toilet paper, condensation, vapour.
Everywhere odours of cabbage and leak,
old frying pans layered with rust,
pantry and kitchens coated with dust,
mice scurrying across bedclothes,
curtain rings pulled over alcoves.
Tenants coping without optimism or hope,
thin-framed, traces
of the house history on their faces.

Saying Goodbye – First Christmas

You sat in a corner staring into silence,
there were photos of grandchildren on the mantelpiece,
everywhere knick-knacks,
the picture rails were hanging with your memories.
Forty-three years is a long time to be together.
The street lamps still cast shadows through the leaded lights
and I am meditating on all the good times
as you did then.
But there are no photos, no ticking clocks,
only a child's voice from next door,
the sounds of the heating as it bursts into life
and junk mail as it lands on the mat.

The Photo Album

Found in Camden Passage, not far from Sadler's Wells,
among the magic lanterns the owner buys and sells
a photo album, gathering dust,
just an idle curiosity,
moments of lives caught within a frame
snapshots of people who have no name.
What can we tell by such a fleeting glance
from their backgrounds, their clothes, their stance,
cashmere, tweeds, leather shoes and pearls?
Perhaps adventurers, daughters of earls,
wives and planters of rubber or tea,
administrators with files to oversee,
civil servants in the diplomatic corps
with home leave taken via Singapore.
The album travelling by sea and on trains
protected from mildew and the rains,
carried overland through mud and the briar,
brought back when they were ready to retire
to Cheltenham, the Cotswolds, the Yorkshire Fells.
Then, how did their photos end up near Sadler's Wells?

Learning the Ropes

Launching with high hopes
being shown the ropes
what we need to know
to run with ebb and flow,
shelter from rough weather,
roll with pitch and sway,
lay at anchor in the bay,
or without moorings,
be content to drift
waiting for the depression to lift.
False starts, bad navigation,
due to our own creation,
may depend on the boat,
how her mariner keeps her afloat.
The skeletal hulks all round,
reminders that timbers once sound
will. one day,
sink back into the mud and clay.

There's no such thing as a free lunch

Treat yourself, an indicator
of lifestyle, choice and taste
as you drink, wear, drive, select
in haste.
At a loss? You needn't be,
buy two get one free.
Money lent at twenty-nine percent,
interest credit free.
Live now pay later.
Are you feeling hale and hearty,
or inadequate? Join the party.
Fill in a questionnaire,
win a prize for a free time share
but beware of publicity.
There's no such thing as a free lunch.

(After Apple Trees and Poplars in the Setting Sun by Pissarro 1830-1903)

Profit from serenity, peace and calm,
friends in the garden, smells of wood-smoke.
There is, as yet, no cause for alarm.

Relax, sip tea, gossip – a delight
in long dress, hat, parasol and cloak.
Profit from serenity, peace and calm.

Apples mature through speckled sunlight,
sounds of laughter, sharing a joke.
There is, as yet, no cause for alarm.

The Old World is courteous and polite,
stable under apple trees and oak.
Profit from serenity, peace and calm,

they'll be no sounds of gunfire tonight,
millions of Europeans under the yoke.
There is, as yet, no cause for alarm,

no power struggles or military might.
History is painted in a brushstroke.
Profit from serenity, peace and calm.
There is, as yet, no cause for alarm.

Grey

Mid-morning, misty November day,
a taxi ride from Leigh-on-Sea
to Rochford village,
the river and its estuary,
bird sanctuary and nesting grounds
the ebb and flow
on mud flats left by an outgoing tide.
In country lanes, hedges in white embroidery
where magpies forage, ivy embraces trees.
The world doesn't stop, muted sounds
in the fog, aircraft taking off,
trains rumbling by.
The Vicar in flowing surplice waiting
in a draughty porch
while candles flicker under Norman vaults.
And the bride wears grey.

Soup Kitchen, Rue de Lille

On the Left Bank as night falls,
reflections light up the Seine,
Notre Dame, the bookstalls,
tourists with bags from boutiques
shopping for chic antiques
add up their losses and gains.
Students from the east,
gardeners from the Tuileries,
the retired, sit down to eat
plates of soup, bread and ham.
Places for only seventy-five,
ten more queue outside,
fruit is pushed into their hands.
They go back to maids-rooms,
bridges, park benches, seats
on the platforms in the Metro.
Parisians drive Mercedes Benz.

There's Just One Slight Problem

In a teashop away from public view
two lovers meeting for a rendezvous,
not noticing others, their looks coded,
language and mannerisms overloaded.
Leaving the first stages of courtship behind,
the future beckoning in the woman's mind,
needing to plan for the rest of her life
to share more than a meal and a beer,
she whispers in her lover's ear
'Have you told your wife?'

Best Friend

That was the deal, a free holiday
to look after the dog while you were away.
'He's such a good soul, there's not much to do,
just a few walks, put food in his bowl,'
EASY, you said.
When you were gone he snarled and snapped,
defended his territory,
attacked the cat, behaved like a cur,
left behind the smell of wet fur.
Our nerves were fraught.
The moment you came through the door,
he was angelic once more.
'He's never behaved that way before.'
You hinted it might be our fault!
PLEASE
don't ask us to look after the dog again!

The 12.30 from Paddington

We are sorry to announce
the late arrival of the First Great Western Service
to Penzance.
We are sorry for the delay due to a police incident.
The world of open sandals,
rustling crisp packets, bags on wheels
and books makes its way to platform 8.
We are sorry to announce
that the 12.30 will be approximately 40 minutes late
and will leave from platform 6.
There are severe delays to this service.
I take my hearing aid out.

After My Grandfather's Funeral

Inside his Edwardian wardrobe,
a dressing gown and cardigan smell of mothballs.
On the bed, the eiderdown shimmers green
over the pink bedspread, a light switch dangles against
the headboard.
Three mirrors reflect my face at different angles,
the last time I will come into his room.
The cut glass dish for collar studs, fruit drops, jar of Vic,
will rest on my dressing table.

Poperinghe*

Dear Uncle Cliff,

I've signed my name again below an Australian's
who with shaking hand writes to his great Uncle Billy,
'I know you'll not read these lines but I'll be back.'
Perhaps you met up at Toc H, rode on horseback,
marched in greatcoats and puttees through the Menin Gate.

The world you left behind of potholes, men drowned,
salients, miles of tunnels underground,
medieval glass and ash from cathedral nave,
wounded, refugees, gave way to fields of wheat, trees.

'Hark,' you'd say, 'the skylark still flies over the spires
of Armentieres and Ypres, their bell towers still chime.'

English signs, Tyne Cot. By a white cross
twelve thousand lay exposed to mists, biting winds, frosts.
Names on a wall : 'I did my best, think of me,'
propped up against a stone. a woman's photo.
Each autumn/spring, bullets, bottles, wellingtons
see the light of day, mementos in the Old Cloth Hall.

I laid a poppy on Otto's grave.

Love from your great-great niece
Jilly

*   Dedicated to the memory of my great-great uncle Sergeant Clifford
Higgins who died on 8th March, 1915, aged 30.

ALAN GRANT

REFLECTIONS OVER TIME

Who was the hero?

I have the name of a man I never knew.
Knew as a father, as a man; one of those special few
Who came quietly to these shores, with uniformed others.
Many feared death, others sought lovers.
Was he like me? Like whom then?
Did he hold me as a child and press his face to mine?
Was I his future, or simply a brief liaison?
My own sons have grown knowing my needs and weaknesses,
What were his? What was he like?
When I lay wondering in the early dawn
Was he also in some lonely barrack thinking of me?
Or had his mind already closed; his heart sealed forever?
I bear the name of a hero, but what does it mean?
Knowing now, that he did survive, and yet
It was my life that passed unseen by him
Father – what did I do?
Where was my hero, when I needed you?

No More Augusts
(A tribute to lost children)

I was born in an August,
And I died in a March.
Children deserve splendid summers,
My guardian angels slept and never knew,
The pain and misery I went through.
Those words of spite, those awful frights
As punches rained, on my empty nights
They saw my face, *they* knew my pain
No lovely summer days, just August sighs with
Locked doors, out of sight, no school, where
Caring friends, shared their bread,
Whilst I lay shivering on my pee-stained bed
Alone, frightened, and unfed,
Waiting for the handle's turn
Then pulled and pushed again, again
Pushed and punched, then locked away for
Another turn, another day of
Water streaming down my throat,
Hands above, until I choke.
Then back to my lonely room, *no eating soon.*
Where were those caring souls,
Whose jobs prescribed *to watch for*
Sights, and sounds and signs
To intervene, to stop my screams,
To hold me close for just one night
To hold my hand, and touch my face
With gentleness and not just rage.
The final blow brought end for me
And shame for them, and yet
No lessons learnt, one child in vain,
Others waiting in the lane.
Summer's not just holidays,
For some it brings neglect, and pain then
More examples, still nothing done.
I was just another one,
Others waiting in the lane.
Others waiting in the lane.

After a While

So now I'm lying in my lonely bed
Wondering, wishing, having not said
What I ought to have, in the life we led.
Not quite the same, this life I now face
Where is the wonder, the life in that race,
To be first, to know your kind grace.
I relished those feelings, our lives inter-twined
Though anxious, uncertain a space in my mind
That never quite needed the solace you now find.
Hoping perhaps in that peaceful surround
Thoughts of our feelings might still abound
Reminding you still of my scent and our sound.
Our moments of passion, moments so brief
That when it was over, both felt the grief
Of knowing deeper feelings that lay just beneath.
Now in the dawn of another dark day
I practice, and practice the words I would say
If your spirit and presence might just come this way.
Whilst knowing deep down that our life is done
I live in denial, yet I *was the one*,
Though no more am I able to bring back the fun.
Making you welcome, making you seek
More from this person, you felt so unique,
In wanting you, loving you, week after week.
Ours was the passion, ours was the pain
In both equal measures we started again
Emotions and wanting, till tears fell like rain.
The silence, then knowing, it's not quite the same
That spectre, that feeling, with no one to blame
Whilst feeling so helpless I whispered your name.
So now I'm lying in my lonely bed
Wondering, wishing, having not said
What I ought to have, in the life we led,
What I ought to have in the life we led.

Street Feet

I look at their feet, when I'm sat on the street, a cardboard cushion easing
the pain
Of sitting, legs crossed, eyes down, no frown, looking down at the ankles
Of those walking past, whilst sitting and waiting for a tinkling plate
No looking up, no looking in, don't let the person see you grin
No bingo game this, eyes down, line and house
My line costs ten quid, and no house in sight, but now it's gone quiet, so
slyly just check
Enough on the blanket to stop feeling wrecked? New feet arrive; nice
polished brogues
Next to his leather, high heels with bare toes, all brightly painted, like my
hopes and dreams
Then down come the coins, and they walk on again, bastards it's foreign-
just 100 yen!
Try changing that at my street exchange, what's wrong with dollars, or
Euros or pounds?
I'm the one sitting with my arse on the ground! Hang on a moment, new
shoes in sight
Old swollen feet, with ankles quite wide, please rest a moment, then open
that purse
Cascade your love down onto my plate, yet all I can hear are words full
of hate
Snide curses above, I'm hers to berate, I know I'm a totally useless shit,
But once I was innocent, sucking on tit, bonding with mother, not full
of nits, like
My dog alongside me, which shivers - It's rain, time to consider;
Shall I increase the pain? Look more pathetic, as hordes pass me by
Hang on a minute I've just got a pie, only half eaten, better than nowt
My dog's bloody started, there's crust on her snout!
Oh let her have it, my time will come, Jesus it's cold, it's right up my
bum,
My cardboard converter is less than my thumb, so pull up the hood and
cover the dog
Here comes a copper, a real PC Plod. He stands and he stares then he
gives me a nod

'Keep bleeding moving you useless great sod'. That's what I *think,* but I
    give him a grin
Cos his beat's nearly over, and he don't want me in.
But the next one is looking for frolics and fun, whilst I, peering down,
    with no clear retreat
Look at his ankles and bloody great feet, Doctor by nature, Doctor
    Martens,
Strapped up and ready, up to his shins, so I move to one side as his kick
    comes in
My brain is more tricky than fixing my chin and, I've always liked soup
    through a cup and a straw, but …
As he falls on his arse pissed as a fart, his boot hits my chest, and stops
    my weak heart.

Veteran's Lament

I know I'm getting older now, some bits are just not working.
Knees that once ran marathons, bend with cortisone lurking,
Eyes that spotted barrack dust, ears that heard a Squaddie's curse,
Now need glasses, hearing aids, or worse.

I know I'm getting older now, don't need to look in mirrors, oh no,
Skin saggy, eyes baggy, hair left long ago,
Steroid enhanced lungs, blue puffer tubes for me.
Have started having trembly hands. Keep spilling cups of tea,

I know I'm getting older now, why can't I just say No?
Stairs no longer bounding places, instead a crimson glow,
Of breathlessness, and heaving chest,
Hang on a minute will you, I need a bloody rest.

I know I'm getting older now, my kids are middle aged.
They call me Sir in shops, seats offered on a bus. Outraged.
Tell Asda staff I'll pack myself, and say "don't make a fuss",
Whilst wondering if I lift it now, does it mean another truss?

I know I'm getting older now, it's like a losing race,
Already bought a funeral plan, and final resting place,
Still thinking on the music, will this one, do the trick?
He's now known as Sir Richard, but is still a total Dick.

I know I'm getting older now, my life was some disgrace.
Am working on the eulogies, if only half' remembered, there'd be
shame upon my face.
Can't reach my feet to cream them, so willing hands entreat,
Need help with socks, wear Velcro shoes, and carefully choose my seat.

I know I'm getting older now, and missing out on chances,
Like tablets blue that start with V and enhance my sexy glances.
Should've read the leaflet first, but listened to a French chum,
Who set me up half rotten, I put them up my bum.

I know I'm getting older now, days start with wind and farts.
Some are planned, some are free, some are neither: was that me?
My brain is still intact though, and mostly near complete,
But found a funny stain last week upon my bedroom sheet

I know I'm getting older now, my gravy runs much faster, so eat with
      bib and tray.
Meals are also changing, with less teeth on display
Can't even tie my shoes up now, even with a bended knee,
Right knee's gone to heaven, left's on "wait and see".

I know I'm getting older now, then, wonder in my lifetime quest,
If it's not easier, to lose the mind, and sod the rest?
It's just waiting for the rest of me, I guess
Knowing nowt, caring less? Hang on a moment, yes, yes, yes.

As the field telephone activated, the middle-aged man reached across and with his khaki-clad arm, lifted the receiver.

"Forward Provost Unit. Sergeant Lenagh." His grip tightened. "One moment Sir, Captain Pentyre's right alongside me."

"Morning Colonel.' There was a hesitation. 'Confirmed? Right Sir. Tomorrow? The warrant is on its way? Thank you, Colonel." Captain Pentyre looked directly at Sergeant Lenagh.

"I can guess, Sir."

"Tomorrow. Warrant signed by the Field Marshal."

"Shall I tell him, or do you want to?"

"You do it please, Sergeant. I'll alert the Padre and organise the squad."

They were in a semi-derelict Belgian farmhouse. The ground floor room with whitewashed walls converted into a basic office, had a passageway leading to an enclosed courtyard. They now used stables as cells. A soldier with a rifle sat on a rough wooden bench next to one with a closed door. He stood up as Sergeant Lenagh approached, and from a ring of keys, selected one before inserting it into the lock.

The cell contained a table, a chair, and against one wall, an army cot. Next to the cot was a washstand with a metal bowl and large jug. There was a small barred window to the rear of the cell. This framed an adjacent tree and as a gentle breeze wafted into the cell, allowed a degree of interrupted sunlight to permeate the room. The flagstone floor, strewn with straw, echoed to Sergeant Lenagh's hobnail boots as he entered. A uniformed body, lying on the bed, stirred.

"Sit up," said the Sergeant gently. At his instruction Private Abraham Bevistein, aged 17, of the Middlesex Regiment placed his feet on the floor then pushed himself upright and buttoned the front of his tunic. His face was thin, very pasty, with distinct black eyebrows, which began to close as he frowned. His eyes closed, then re-opened, moving from side to side. He took several deep breaths, then gripped the side of the cot as the Sergeant spoke.

"The decision of the Courts Martial is confirmed. The decision will be implemented at dawn tomorrow."

"What does that mean, Sarge? Decision implemented?"

"What it means, son, is having been found guilty of desertion you will be executed. Can't make it any easier than that. I don't know what you were expecting. It's the Court's decision."

The soldier interrupted. "Look, Sarge, I know you've only known me a little while, but they never listened to me. Tried to tell 'em what really happened. Had this young officer; supposed to talk for me in court, but he hardly said anything. Colonel kept staring at him. It was all over in twenty minutes. They just wouldn't listen. It's not fair, Sarge. Not fair."

As he spoke, the Sergeant saw a tear trickling down Abraham's face.

"Look, son. There's no appeal. It's final. I've read some of the court papers." He paused. "This is all I can do. *You* tell me what happened. At least you'll know someone heard."

The Sergeant picked up the chair and placed it alongside the cot. He withdrew a packet of cigarettes from his tunic pocket and offered one to Abraham.

"No thanks, Sarge," Abraham paused. "Me and Herbert. Private Burden, we went to the same school and joined up together. Both of us were only 16, but we thought we'd try it on, pretend we were older. Got away with it. Chose the Middlesex 'cos of my uncle. Anyway, we were sent out on observation. Found this shell-hole. It was almost dry, not like the trenches, always sodding wet. We'd been there for about an hour when Jerry started lobbing shells over, getting closer and closer. Didn't know what to do.

"Then Herbert suddenly stood up, said he was going to run back to our lines, but as he did so, a shell landed right alongside. Massive shrapnel. Next thing I'm lying on my back in the mud with Herbert lying across me. Horrible. His tunic ripped open, and he's holding his stomach in. There was blood everywhere, and he was screaming. His face was all twisted, and a bit of his jaw was gone. Tried to get him off me, but every time I moved, he screamed again. Kept calling for his mum, Emily."

"How long were you there?"

"Couple of hours. Herbert crying, screaming. Then he paused, and his body went all funny like and I knew he was dead; my best mate, dead. I pushed him away. Picked up my rifle and took his as well, then crawled back to our trenches, shouting out the password. But it had also hit them. It was murder down there, people panicking all over the place, wounded shouting out; so, I just kept on walking, right out of the trench."

"What about your rifles?"

"Dropped them somewhere. I was sick of it all. Night after night. Weren't due to be relieved for another week. I just kept walking, passing dead blokes all lined up waiting to be taken away. Saw other mates amongst them. Sarge, Herbert was only 16, and I'm just 17."

"What did you do?"

"Found this barn about half a mile away. Just went in and sat there trembling, crying, for hours, hearing Herbert's screams in my head. Then fell asleep. Next thing the Red Caps are shaking me. Telling me I'm a coward." Abraham reached out and grasped the Sergeant's hand. *"I'm not a coward, Sarge.* Put me back on the front line. *Now. Right now.* I'll show you. Put me back, *please."*

"It's too late for that, son. I can't stop what's got to happen, but I'll make bloody sure others know about you. I promise. Now, do you want to see a Padre?"

"Is there a Rabbi?"

"No; not on this sector of the front. The Padre's work across all faiths. Yes?" Abraham nodded.

"Sarge, can I ask you a question?" He paused. 'Will they still send my pay to my Mum? She's got a couple of kids to care for. With Dad dead, I'm the only earner."

"I'll make sure of it.' Abraham looked up, his eyes watering as his lips trembled. He looked directly into the Sergeant's face.

"Will you be there tomorrow?' The Sergeant nodded, before touching Abraham on the shoulder and hurrying out of the cell. As he entered the office, Captain Pentyre looked up.

"Bastards. Those absolute bastards at HQ. Does the Field Marshal have a clue what is going on down here?" The Sergeant pointed towards the cells, his voice emphatic. "That poor sod doesn't deserve a bullet. He's just a child. I met the RSM from the Royal Irish yesterday. They've just had a casualty *aged 14 years of age.* What are we doing, Sir?"

"Calm down, Sergeant. Please." There was a pause. "I fully appreciate your anger. This entire war is immoral, but you and I have a job to do. There will be casualties in many ways, not just on the battlefield, and not just with the innocence of youth. The squad has arrived. They're from three different regiments, so I would suggest you brief them. Padre is on his way. Let's do *our* duty properly, at least."

Sergeant Lenagh walked into a nearby room, used as a dormitory. The group of soldiers looked up expectantly.

"I'm the Provost Sergeant. Appreciate you've been detailed off, but this is what is to happen."

"*I volunteered,*" said a burly soldier, dressed in the distinctive khaki and dark tartan uniform of the Black Watch. "*I don't have a problem being here. Hate fucking cowards.*"

The Sergeant walked directly up to him.

"Well, my kilted friend, let me tell you something. I would be *proud* to be the father of the lad we're executing in a few hours time. Proud. Do you hear me?" No response. "*Do you?*"

The soldier nodded sheepishly. Sergeant Lenagh continued.

"Once the prisoner is secured to the chair and blindfolded, you will march in single file and each take a rifle from the rack. All rifles, with one exception will be loaded with live ammunition. I will give you the order to take up position. When I say aim, address your rifle at the white patch on the prisoner's chest. I will then say fire. Understood? Right be ready for 0700."

There was a weak sunlight breaking through the adjacent trees as the Sergeant entered the cell. He carried a tin mug.

"Drink this son." Abraham coughed as the whisky entered his throat. His body was visibly trembling.

"Right, son. It's time. I'll make it as quick as possible. I *know* you're not a coward. Here's your chance to prove it to them out there. Stand up, put your hands behind you."

"Sorry, Sarge. *I've just pissed myself.*"

The Sergeant paused. "*No, you haven't son.* I just brought you a brew of tea, and *I* spilled it. Right? Now. Hands."

Having quickly secured the leather strap, he spoke softly to Abraham.

"Show them what you're made of, soldier. *Quick march!*"

Abraham walked swiftly into the courtyard, moved towards the heavy wooden chair and without hesitation, sat down. He glanced around the courtyard, then nodded as the guard approached and secured a strap around his chest.

The Sergeant walked directly in front of him, wrapped a blindfold across his eyes, then pinned a white square to his chest. He leant forward.

"*I'm proud of you, soldier.* God bless you, son "

Abraham's chest rose as the Sergeant turned towards the squad.

A DIFFERENT PERSPECTIVE

Days merged imperceptibly with one another. We'd been wanting to make this journey for several years, and then one day, and quite unexpectedly, a company reorganisation brought redundancy, with a decent settlement. After some hesitation, and with both of us wanting to take the initiative, somehow the suggestion was being discussed, tentatively at first, then with increasing enthusiasm and momentum. Finally we were here, with our newly built hotel with a private balcony, facing onto the most beautiful sandy bay I'd ever seen. Daily and frequent walks became a much loved routine.

I stood on the beach watching the gentle breeze ruffling John's hair. His prematurely greying locks resting against his thin tanned face, provided a backdrop for his lovely piercing blue eyes. He was concentrating deeply on his sketchpad, tanned hands moving rhythmically across the surface, as he regularly looked up at the horizon, and then translated the images. The sea was imperceptibly moving towards him, and I knew that very shortly he would have to pick up the folding chair and retreat back towards me.

John seemed totally immersed in his surroundings, although he responded occasionally to a stray dog, which had recently appeared and singled him out for attention. It was carrying a dark, discoloured stick in its mouth and laid it playfully down at John's feet It backed off a few paces tail wagging expectantly, then yelped excitedly as he reached down, picked up the stick and threw it along the edge of the water. Anticipating the direction of his throw, the dog scampered away, quickly retrieved it and ran back to begin the process all over again.

This behaviour went on for ages, which I found quite surprising because John had never really been a doggy sort of person, and usually preferred the company of cats, where his gentle manner and tactile needs were more fulfilled. Eventually, even John got fed up and managed to convince the dog that he'd thrown the stick in one direction, whilst in fact hiding it underneath his seat. The dog looked puzzled, and for a while ran back and forth along the beach before seemingly getting bored and trotting off towards the adjacent road.

John stood up and shading his eyes with one hand, slowly traversed the surroundings. He settled on a particular view, moved his chair back several yards to avoid the lapping water, and then resumed his drawing. To an onlooker he would have appeared to be totally at peace, a relaxed holidaymaker. As his wife for 30 years, I knew nothing could be further from the truth.

He was still deeply grieving and traumatised by the loss of our darling Jenny. Whilst his tears had lessened, they now fell in some secret place. From the moment Jenny was born, there'd been a magic between them. A special affinity, which epitomised itself in a deeply loving father and daughter relationship.

It had been a difficult pregnancy. We'd both given up on the idea that we could ever have a child of our own. Tests, disappointment, further tests and more demoralising news, with a clock that was inexorably ticking away. Then those first few days of uncertainty, anxiety and initial awareness. Small subtle changes to my body, and odd feelings. Such odd feelings. A growing optimism, which initially I didn't want to share with anyone. I wanted to be absolutely sure, so it was nearly three months before I decided to tell John.

He was looking tired when he came home from the office, and sat down wearily in the lounge. This was the moment that Sam, our Siamese cat, had been waiting for all day. She emerged from her favourite daytime resting place, on the ledge adjacent to the window, where she basked in the sunlight. Without seeking any permission, she jumped quickly onto John's lap, curled herself around the contours of his body and fell asleep. All day I'd wondered how he might take the news, and had done some gentle rehearsals.

He didn't leap up and punch the air, nor shout out exuberantly, but his whole being changed. It was as if a gentle light suddenly flickered and grew within his eyes, before slowly spreading across his whole face. There was a subtle, then more repetitive and evident shake of his head, then a developing smile, which quickly transformed his air of tiredness into one of joy. A trickle of tears ran down his face. He sniffed, and then gently lifted Sam into his arms, and for a moment buried his face deep within her soft welcoming fur. Sam protested gently, as she always did when her sleep was disturbed; responding with that oh so familiar, unique Siamese growl.

The following months were a blur of tests, anxiety, growing excitement and absolute anticipation across our whole family and friends. Then one wet and thundery evening, just before midnight and with a cry of such piercing presence, that it could be heard throughout the ward, she was finally there. Our long awaited, adorable and so unique Jenny.

John was absolutely besotted with her. There were times, when even I felt an occasional twinge of jealousy, as he calmed the most fractious and fearsome temper tantrum. Laying her tiny frame across his shoulder, he would gently pat and rub her back until she was calm, before other than for the occasional whimper, she'd sleep.

To suggest that Jenny was idolised would be an understatement. She became the focal point of our lives. We were determined to give her every opportunity and experience possible; encouraging her development, reinforcing every achievement, and daily feeling blessed and in awe that she was such a lovely and responsive child. Early school days merged into adolescence, which became a blue of university examinations culminating in the realisation that our darling daughter was now a young woman.

She strode purposefully across the podium to collect her degree watched by two middle aged people with watery eyes and an enormous sense of pride, and then gave us a shy little wave as she descended the steps on the other side. During her university days she'd been able to remain at home, so apart from the occasional holiday or degree pursuit, our lives had been entwined for over 20 years.

Jenny told me first, about her desire to take a gap year and travel abroad before seeking employment. We agreed how she would broach the subject with John. I don't know if he had any sense of foreboding, although he was strangely quiet in the early months of her absence. I knew that he was missing her as dreadfully as I did. For both of us Jenny was more than a daughter, rather a genuine friend, and for me especially, a confidant.

She kept in touch regularly during her time in the various countries she visited. Phone calls from Ecuador, emails from San Francisco, postcards from Cape Town, and occasional letters with obscure stamps from diverse parts of the world. Jenny embraced all the experiences with her usual eagerness and appetite for learning. We were not a religious family, but gradually John and I realised, that

Jenny was not only on a journey of discovery in terms of the physical world, she was also exploring her own spirituality.

It was not surprising therefore to receive a much awaited, rather bulky envelope in which she described working in an orphanage in Thailand, run by Buddhist monks, and that she had decided to adopt their faith. Knowing that she'd already made such a decision was quite comforting when the other devastating news arrived.

The stray dog had reappeared and was approaching John again. There were dozens of couples on the beach, and it seemed odd that it seemed to be consistently seeking us out. I hesitated before speaking.

"John. Do you know that in the Buddhist faith, when someone dies they can be reincarnated as an animal?"

He looked at me quizzically, before reaching under his chair and picking up the stick again.

"What are you suggesting?"

"Well, it seems strange that the dog has sought us out on several occasions, despite the fact that the beach has dozens of people on it, and especially as this is the actual place Jenny was last seen before the Tsunami arrived."

He turned away briefly, then reached out and touched my face with his hand.

"I think it's time to go back to the hotel," he said gently. Then he paused and turned.

"It would be nice though." And in one movement threw the stick into the air and shouted:

"Come on Jenny. Fetch!"

As the stick arched slowly, tumbling across the sky, before falling into the water, the dog was nowhere to be seen. John turned back to me, and I could see a wetness in his eyes. We looked at one another without speaking for a few moments, then he reached down and began to pack up his drawing materials and canvas.

"John wait. Can I see how far you've progressed the painting." Without waiting for a response, I moved towards him, and gently pulled it out from under his arm. The image of the bay, with the golden sands, palm trees, and gently rolling white topped surf was quite magnetic. In the forefront, he had already begun to develop the outline of a familiar figure, in a remembered stance.

"Will the accused please address the Bench. You have heard the evidence against you in respect of you behaving in an unseemly and offensive manner in the auditorium of Plymouth Pavilions on the night of 1ˢᵗ October 1991. I note you are not represented, so in your own words how do you respond?"

"Well Sir, I'd been looking forward to the Queen rock concert for months. Hours standing in the freezing cold, then the precious ticket, that I clutched to my chest, before putting it safely away in my bedside cabinet. Although I live on my own, I even locked it. Most Friday nights, Codi the tenant of the next flat and I take it in turns to cook a meal. She likes to experiment and certainly exceeded herself that weekend. The night before the concert, I had my first Indian Codi curry.

"It was about 2 o'clock in the morning when I first rushed to the toilet. Then all the next day I was up and down like a yo-yo, dreading the next pulsing surge in my stomach, which had ballooned. I had a stark choice; try and sell my Queen ticket, or hope that I could get through the performance. My body was exhausted; surely the effect of Bombay belly could not continue to haunt me over 18 hours later. I decided to chance it.

"Queen was brilliant and started their gig with 'I'm Going Slightly Mad'. So was I. Despite trying to put the continuing turmoil in my bowels, out of my mind, I realised I had to visit the loo again. Choosing a moment just as Freddy Mercury disappeared for a swift half, I made a dash. I looked like a principal male dancer in the Royal Ballet, as I scooted down the corridor with my buttocks tightly clenched and toes pointing outwards. There was one cubicle left, so I stumbled into it and signalled my relief with a desperate sigh and a fart as the toilet seat slammed down beneath my gluteus maximus.

"I knew immediately I'd made a serious mistake, but it was too late. I could hear the arena crowd getting excited again, yet in my panic, I'd not lowered my trousers before I sat down. It was becoming even noisier in the auditorium. Freddie must be back. I faced a stark choice. Deal with my loss of dignity, or miss the Queen concert.

"I tucked my trousers in my socks and walked or rather sloshed back out. As I got closer to the stage, gaps in the crowd appeared all over the place. A security guard seemed to be measuring the crowd pressure, moving people on and paying particular attention to me. I was just starting to jump around to Freddy again, when this woman ran up and hit me with her umbrella. Started swearing at me and gagging. Then I was arrested and missed the second half. Not fair."

"Let's have a look at you," said his other, brushing her fingers through his dark brown hair. "Are your shoes clean?"

"Yes Mum, done them they're ready, everything's fine."

Whilst Ian enjoyed being touched, he was embarrassed at the current close attention.

"You look smashing, son. The blazer is perfect. Are you OK? Ready to go? Don't be nervous. I'm proud of you. Don't forget – you're special, not only to your Mum, but to the whole of your last school. Remember, you were the only one to pass the 11+. Well done."

Ian nodded, knowing that the next few hours would be a turning point in his life. If it was raining, he could at least cover up the new blazer. His raincoat had come from a jumble sale at the local community hall last Saturday. It was dark blue, with a half belt; old and worn, but better than a light blue blazer. They never wore blazers on this estate. Ian knew that once his former school mates saw him, they would all be laughing. His mother seemed to have forgotten the quartered cap, then she looked at him.

"Put the cap on son. Let's make sure it fits."

Ian opened the brown paper bag, his name already stencilled on the inner lining. He put it on his head. The light blue quartered cap with centralised house badge dominated his whole face. Boys didn't wear caps on this estate, only old men, with fags in their mouths and war worn, wrinkled faces. Men wore the same cap; flat, checked, greasy and smelling of tobacco and most seemed to cough a lot in the early mornings.

His mother looked at him for a moment, before tugging the cap down and to the side. She stepped back and looked at him. Her face had a look of real satisfaction, although Ian noticed a wetness to her eyes.

"You'll do," she whispered. "Off you go now and catch your bus. I'm working late again today, so hope to be home right after you. Pick up the kids and put the tea on, if you get in first."

As she spoke, he saw tears welling. As a post-war, single mother of three, his mother only cried in private. Ian knew his life as an eleven-year-old wartime evacuee, and top pupil at the Junior school on a newly built, 1950s council estate, was about to change forever.

"Good luck, bruv," said his younger sister, holding in her arms, an even younger brother mumbling through his dummy, whilst holding his arms out for a kiss, his urine soaked, smelly nappy, clinging to his podgy thighs. Ian's mother intervened and lifted the baby into her arms.

"Right you two. Let's get you ready for the nursery. Till tonight, son. Good luck. I love you." She paused. "We all do."

He drew a deep breath and opened the front door. It was a quarter of a mile to the bus stop. The Woolworth's satchel was slung across his shoulder. It contained his former Headmaster's gift of white gym shoes and a compass. These lay upon a small bag of yesterday's still fresh, bread rolls, with some paper and pencils stolen from his mother's office. In a brown paper bag, also purchased from Woolworth's with his own pocket money, was an unopened, unused plastic fountain pen and a small bottle of black ink.

Ian thought to himself that it would have been nice to have a father watch him go to grammar school for the first time; he paused, shrugged and began his walk. The high hedgerow of their neighbour's garden gave him his first opportunity. He took off the quartered cap, rolled it up, and stuffed it into a side pocket of his satchel. Leaving at seven-thirty to catch the first of three buses to school had distinct advantages. Most of his former schoolmates were still in bed. The bus befuddled with smoke and sweaty coughing adults, had a young passenger intent on taking up his place at an elite Grammar School in the nearest town some 8 miles away.

As his final bus approached the Grammar school, Ian watched several cars discharging other uniformed pupils, who entered the school grounds. It was 1952 and whilst on his estate, cars were a rarity and driven by Spivs or sales reps, many children seemed to have been driven to this school.

He descended from the upper deck of the bus, retrieved his quartered cap from the satchel and pulled it onto his head. The final hundred yards from the bus stop to the school gates seemed an eternity. Pulling at his loose fitting but new grey socks, which barely reached the bottom of his short trousers, he rubbed the front of his shoes on the reverse of each leg, and walked towards the gates.

A group of larger older boys were waiting on the pavement; dressed in similar school blazers, yet menacing in appearance, some with adolescent pock marked faces, all intent on scrutinising new entrants to the school.

'Here's another one,' said a member of the group, his oafish features focused on the approach of Ian.

"Oh hell, my socks are falling down again," Ian thought, pulling at the cheap grey woollen sleeves which encased his spindly white legs, whilst trying to balance his school satchel. He tried to avert his gaze from the group at the gates.

"Where do you think you're going?" said the lead oaf, moving out in front of him, his eyes on the brand-new blazer and cheap satchel.

"School please. I'm new here. This is my first day. Where do I go? Please?"

"Well, you can take that thing off for a start," said the questioner, ripping the quartered cap from Ian's head. He realised that none of the older boys were wearing caps, although they all wore the standard school blazer with various house badges attached.

"Now bugger off."

Ian watched his cap being jammed across the spikes of an adjacent school fence, joining several others in a bizarre montage. As he did so, there was a sudden tugging and ripping on the pockets of his blazer. His jacket, purchased by a special grant from the Education Department, available only to families living in poverty, was damaged.

"Piss off, you bastards!" Ian screamed, before running through the school gates, tears rolling down his cheeks. In the sanctuary of the school entrance hall he stopped. His hands shook, and his breathing was becoming difficult.

"Now what?" he thought, before looking down at his torn blazer and becoming very anxious. His palms were already sweaty, so he tried to wipe them on his hair, and tidy it before straightening the new school tie which was tight. He'd never worn a tie before and had relied on his mother to use the relevant knot.

"What if it comes undone?" he thought to himself. 'Mum will go daft when she finds out about this, and that'll make it worse for me. I'm sure of that." He looked towards the school gates, and the group of older boys now dispersing. Ian walked into the vaulted main hall of the school in a dishevelled state. A school prefect was standing inside the main corridor and called him over.

"You as well?"

Ian nodded, looking down at his shoes, and realising that once again his loose grey socks had fallen down to his ankles. The prefect reached out his hand and adjusted Ian's tie. "Some of us have been there. Like you. Ignore them twats. It only lasts a day. They only get away with it because of some stupid school tradition, which has got out of hand. My name's Tony. If you have any more problems, come to me. I'm around here before classes start. Your room is there on the left 14B.' Tony paused. 'Good luck, kid.''

As he entered Room 14B, there was a serried row of desks with metal frames, and thick wooden surfaces. Most desks had occupants. Facing them was a large blackboard, with a larger desk in front. There, sat an elderly man wearing a dark blue suit, under a black gown checking a register. As Ian closed the door behind him, the man showed with his finger he should approach him.

As he did so, Ian recognised the familiar smell of tobacco which had permeated the three buses he had caught that morning. Without apparently seeing he damage to his blazer, or the agitated state that Ian was in, the man spoke.

"I'm Mr Parkinson, your tutor and teacher of the English Language. Name?"

Ian responded and explained what had happened.

"Your name is all I asked for. Other issues can wait. Name?" Ian responded. The teacher pointed to a desk next to a window. "Sit there."

His arrival in class completed the registration process. Mr Parkinson spoke at length about school hours, lesson arrangements, procedures, assemblies and worship, meal routines, even the values and history of this elite all male Grammar School, commending some of its most successful and well-known former scholars. He never referred to Ian's earlier attempt to explain what had happened to him.

The rest of the day was a blur of classroom changes, lesson schedules, and being overwhelmed by the sheer size and numbers of other pupils, some of whom although uniformed like him, were as sixth-formers, already adults, needing to shave regularly. It sank in. From being top of the pile at his Junior school, passing the 11+, on his own and being a local estate hero he now faced a massive challenge.

The three-bus journey home went well. Ian got off at an earlier stop prior to collecting his younger sister and brother from the Council nursery, and pushing them both home. When he stepped off the bus, he removed his recovered but damaged quartered cap, and put on his raincoat. The pavements were quiet.

On some adjacent grass, former classmates from his Junior school, acknowledged his presence, with a few waves, before returning to their game of football. Their "goalposts" were piles of jackets, coats, clothing and satchels. His heavy satchel was already crammed with homework.

After settling his sister and brother down with a drink and biscuit, Ian walked into the kitchen. On the cooker was a heavy saucepan containing prepared vegetables and mince. In the adjacent cupboard he found a box of matches, struck one and lit the gas burner beneath the pan. As he did so, he heard the front door open.

His mother instinctively sensed his tension. As she saw the damage to his blazer he knew his mother would react. Explaining the day's events she simply reached out and pulled him towards her. "I wish I could have been with you on your first day," she said, "but I need to work Ian and with your sister being sick two weeks ago they were getting funny about me taking any more time off. Do you understand?" Ian nodded.

"I'm not letting this go though. The Council won't give us another grant till next year."

He was unsure how the school would respond to being challenged on what seemed to be a traditional ritual for new boys. Next day he found out. A summons to the office of the Headmaster, Mr Ackerman. There was a distinct coolness in his manner. He had a letter in his hand addressed to his mother. "Please tell your mother that following her telephone call this morning, the School welfare funds will provide a new cap and blazer. This letter is the authority to the school uniform supplier."

"Yes Sir. Thank you, Sir. Sorry but I …"

Mr Ackerman raised his hand. "Enough. Put this letter away and make sure your mother gets it tonight. Now go back to your class and let this be the end."

However, five years of misery lay ahead.

I'd just come back from my walkabout when I realised something was different. I'd been to the park first. Love it there, especially in the Spring, flowers emerging, and bird's nests full of young fledglings, learning to fly.

Opposite my home, was a large van. People were unloading lots of furniture. The house had been empty for months. The front door was open, so I strolled over and peeked in. Wow. My new neighbour was an absolute cracker. Slim, blonde hair with brown streaks. I peed on the doorstep.

Would she fancy the local tom? she meowed. Soon know.

JACK HORNE

BEACH BUM

I spluttered and my teacup rattled on its saucer. "What did you just say, dear?"

Without looking up from her knitting, Vera repeated: "This year, I shall walk up and down the beach in my birthday suit."

Walter's eyes looked huge, magnified by his glasses. He scratched his threadbare head and studied his wife. "Do you think that's … a good idea?" he asked, fiddling with his tie. "I mean …"

Vera's blue eyes twinkled as she looked up at us both. "Why not? I'll be ninety. Life's for living." She continued knitting.

I glanced around the familiar cluttered lounge, while I struggled to think of something to say. Even Vera said the chintz was overpowering, but Walter loved it. The creaking of my friends' wooden rocking chairs, the click-clack of Vera's knitting needles and the ticking of the grandfather clock seemed very loud. I finally asked "Is the beach full of naturists?"

"What, people who study wildlife?" Walter asked.

I sighed. "Nudists."

Vera shrugged and unbuttoned her rainbow-coloured cardigan. "I don't know. Who cares? At my age, one learns to do one's own thing, Mavis. You'll be the same some day."

"I'm not far behind you," I said, taking another homemade coconut bun from the plate on the coffee table. "I'm nearly eighty-nine."

Vera sniggered. "Well, I can't imagine you on a nudist site. You wouldn't know where to look."

I felt myself flush. "Neither would you."

Walter chuckled. "Oh, she would. Nothing embarrasses Vera, you should know that by now."

I sipped my tea, only vaguely listening to Vera's smutty nudist jokes and Walter's chortles. Was she really planning to parade naked along the local beach? I had a sudden vision of her riding along the sands on a donkey, like Age Concern's very own Lady Godiva. No, surely even Vera wouldn't do that.

I glanced at the photographs on the mantelpiece: Vera skydiving, abseiling, running a marathon and wing-walking on a Tiger Moth biplane. She had done something daring on each of her milestone birthdays. Her ninetieth wouldn't be an exception.

Walter offered me another bun. I eyed the plate, biting my bottom lip. He was good at making them, but I really shouldn't have a third.

"Go on," he said. "Just another won't make any difference."

Vera nodded, her ginger wig askew. "It's impossible to tell how fat you really are, with all that clobber you wear."

"I feel the cold." I sniffed and changed the subject …

*

At home, I ran a bath and viewed my plump nakedness in the full-length mirror. Not everyone could be Venus or Adonis. With her thin legs and large bosom, Vera reminded me of a bird, but she was happy to bare all on a crowded beach.

Soaking in the steaming lavender-scented water, I thought about Vera's birthday. I'd always been too serious. I wouldn't even join her in karaoke, but it was time to change. I'd buy a thong and strip off on the beach beside her. I smiled, imagining her surprise. Maybe I'd even get carried away by the moment and remove the thong too …

*

Vera's birthday was a sunny day, the sort that draws crowds to the beach. Sunbathers were everywhere and a group of teenagers were playing football. Vera and I strolled by the sea.

I stepped out of my sandals and woollen tights, the waves lapping my feet. I wondered when she'd remove her old tartan outfit. Side-eyeing her, I shrugged off my cardigan. She didn't seem to notice, until I removed my blouse.

"Are you feeling all right?" she asked, and then stared at my lime green thong as I pulled down my tweed skirt.

Ignoring the sniggering sunbathers around us, I unclipped my brassiere. I felt free as I swung it overhead and tossed it behind me. Someone cheered.

Vera looked concerned. "Have you been out in the sun for too long?"

"I'm feeling wonderful. As you've always said, who cares what anyone else thinks!"

A dog ran past with my bra in its mouth.

110

"I can't wait to tell Walter!" Vera shrieked with laughter. "What's got into you? I've always loved you like a sister, but I thought you were rather boring. I didn't have any ambitions left but you've outdone anything I did."

I swallowed. My mouth was suddenly dry. "But you said you were going to completely strip off."

"Eh?" Vera frowned and then giggled. "Ohhh, my birthday suit. Walter thinks it's too expensive to wear on the beach, but sand and salt water, even ice cream and seagulls' muck, won't really do much harm."

I looked at the red tartan dress and matching jacket that, yes, she always wore on her birthday …

And then, for the first time in my life, I threw my head back and laughed.

On Sunday November 13th 1892, as the rain pelted down outside, the evening service at St Peter's church, in Peter Tavy, was in full swing.

Reverend Dr Bryant delivered a rousing sermon and the choir sang beautifully, accompanied by 22-year-old William Rowe on the church organ. But some of the younger members of the congregation were not entirely full of peace and goodwill.

Emma Doidge, a pretty 17-year-old chorister, had persuaded her brother William to protect her on the way to and from the church. She had been bombarded with unwanted love letters from the bell-ringer, 21-year-old William Williams, and he had become increasingly abusive.

After the service, while the congregation gathered outside, William Doidge approached Williams and told him to leave her alone. She already had a boyfriend, William Rowe, the church organist, and didn't want to have anything to do with Williams. The rejected suitor's response to this was that he would "knock Emma's head off."

Doidge immediately pulled off his jacket and raised his fists at the bell-ringer, challenging him to a fight, but Williams declined, saying he didn't want to spoil his best suit. Instead, he offered to meet the next day when he would be wearing his miller's work clothes. Williams then stormed off down the lane to the village.

Emma told her brother and younger sister, Elizabeth, to walk on home to Coxtor Farm ahead of her and Rowe, as the danger had passed when William Williams left.

As they reached home William and Elizabeth heard the sound of four gunshots ringing out over the fields. They rushed off in the direction of the gunfire. Nothing could have prepared them for what they found.

Only 500 yards from their home they found Emma and William Rowe sprawled on the road, blood flowing from head wounds. The hedges bordering the lane were splattered with blood. Emma had been shot in the forehead and probably died instantly, but Rowe had been shot in the back of the head and part of his brain was spilling out. Miraculously, he was still alive.

Emma's lifeless body was taken to a neighbour's farm and Rowe was rushed to his parents' home in the village of Peter Tavy in the farmer's trap. Reverend Bryant, who had been called to the scene, rode into the village to fetch a doctor, who, after examining Rowe, said there was no hope. The organist died at nine o'clock the following morning.

The murder weapon, a common pin-fire type gun, had been left in the lane, and the police found that four cartridges had been expended.

William Williams was missing, but two and a half hours later, his father received a message that his oldest son was hiding out in a cottage at Harford Bridge.

The police stormed the small dwelling to find Williams, his clothes dripping wet, with two bullet wounds to his head – but still alive.

He was taken to Tavistock cottage hospital, where it was discovered that he had attempted suicide three times that day. The first bullet had missed his left temple, grazed his forehead and passed through the brim of his hat. The second had passed through his right eye and was embedded in his ear.

The double-killer had then thrown himself into the River Tavy – but panicked at the last minute and scrambled from the river to ask for help at a nearby farmer's home.

The farmer and his daughter didn't recognise Williams at first, because he was covered in blood from his head wounds. The girl gave Williams a cup of tea, and later said that he had refused to explain his shocking appearance.

The bullet in Williams's shattered right eye was removed at Tavistock hospital and found to match those used in the murders of Emma Doidge and William Rowe. Before he would talk to the police, Williams, who was reported to be suffering from "great mental anguish", asked to see his parents.

Williams then told the police that on November 8th, he had bought the gun at Blanchard's, an ironmonger's shop in Tavistock. Blanchard often sold rifle cartridges to him and, therefore, wasn't suspicious.

Five days later, Williams said, he took the gun to church with him and, after the service and his confrontation with Emma's brother, hid behind a hedge in the lane. He watched William and Elizabeth Doidge pass him on their way home, but waited until Emma appeared with her boyfriend.

He went on to say that he grabbed Emma's left arm, ripping the sleeve of her dress, and shot her at point-blank range. Rowe tried to escape, but Williams chased him and shot him 12 yards from Emma's body.

Williams then attempted to shoot himself on the spot. The first bullet knocked his hat off, where it fell beside Rowe's hat. After firing into his own eye, he dropped the gun, and made for the river.

On March 9th 1893, the Western Morning News reported that Williams' plea of insanity at his trial was rejected and that the jury had taken just 10 minutes to deliver a verdict of wilful murder. The judge told the jury they would have been wanting in their duty if they had found otherwise, as he had never heard of a more cruel or more deliberate murder.

Emma's father, John, the churchwarden, said he believed Williams had written to Emma and that she'd simply refused to have anything to do with him. However, a lifelong friend of Emma's told the newspaper that Williams and Emma had known one another very well and Emma had written to the love-sick miller and told him to leave her alone.

However well they knew each other, it was Emma's spurning of him that turned William Williams into a cold-hearted killer. And he was hanged at Exeter prison on March 28th 1893.

The Loneliness of the Long-Distance Singer

They sent her off to outer space
And told her, 'Practice there.'
They couldn't bear her screeching voice;
She thought she sung with flair.

A friendly spacecraft picked her up
As she was floating round;
They thought she was a lovely girl
But couldn't stand the sound.

Her *Casta Diva* truly dire;
Her *Vissi d'arte* sad;
She dreamed she'd be a superstar
But drove the spacecrew mad.

They dropped her off and shot away -
I guess she's drifting still,
Attempting tone deaf *Un bel di*,
Unheard, her voice as shrill.

Alone, she hits the highest notes
But no one has to hear;
They know she may return some day:
The music lovers' fear.

But till that day our singer wails;
And here on Earth all peace prevails.

Misty Moorland

I crossed the moor one murky morning.
It looked like a partially painted page:
grey-white with just a little green at the base,
but instead of filling with colour
it gradually grew greyer … greyer.

And I was soon wandering
in a blank canvas world.

The fog foul-smelling,
like burnt suede in a boiled-dry pan;
sounds of ponies, cattle and sheep
muffled, muted.

As I turned three hundred and sixty degrees
it seemed I stood in a circle:
a ring of grass in the greyness
was all I could see.
Myths came to mind and I imagined a fairy ring.

Fantasy turned to fear when I realised I was lost …
… lost … lost …

NICK INGRAM

SHABBY CHIC 2022

... Summer ...

And so these quiet wasted summer days
pass by in occluded emotions of
regret and silence, numbered by the
calendar, framed as a still picture,
a series of pointillist dots dabbed onto
the texture of the canvas. I can no
longer celebrate this summer, this shifting
season of a few months – I have lost the
ability to be disappointed.
A low caresses the sky; there will be
thunder this afternoon. Just maybe I
don't want to be civilised anymore:
I just want to be feral screaming at
the sun.

... N – E – U ...

Voices. Voices. Voices.
Too many voices.
Scatological.
Scattering.
Empty. Void.
Post essence.
No slumber.
Thought.
Cast off.
Cast away.
Not Reading.
Non-books.
Poetry.
Neu-poetry.
N – E – U poetry.

… Stiff Whiskey Cock …

The Lavender Orpington walked into
the bar: suddenly all the cocks went stiff.
There is, maybe, something of the romantic
left within me; I thought it had gone.
The tiredness tends to seep in through the joints:
in-between the mussel. Pudding is
never boring. Vegetables are always
a little dull to talk to, at least,
unlike puddings, they don't shout at you. Freud
would have had it no other way. Whiskey
please! Free verse can be perverse but any
perversion is always an exquisite
pleasure. Windows™: I hate Windows™ and their
updates! I hate up-loading. I hate down-
loading. I want to disconnect, only
connect, only connect, connect only,
only connect, connect, connect, connect only,
only. Was this the silence we were all
born from, this freedom, this passion, this flood
of onomatopoeia banging on
the door? This is how you feel when your word
means nothing at all: therefore, we begin
once more. Hash tag movements never change a
thing. Only people movements can change things.
Roll D20, misses Armour Class 3, even
with bonuses: the poetry monster
survives to fight another day. In
certain schools of thought contemporary
poetry is only valid if it
ticks the right boxes! Tick scratch tick tick.

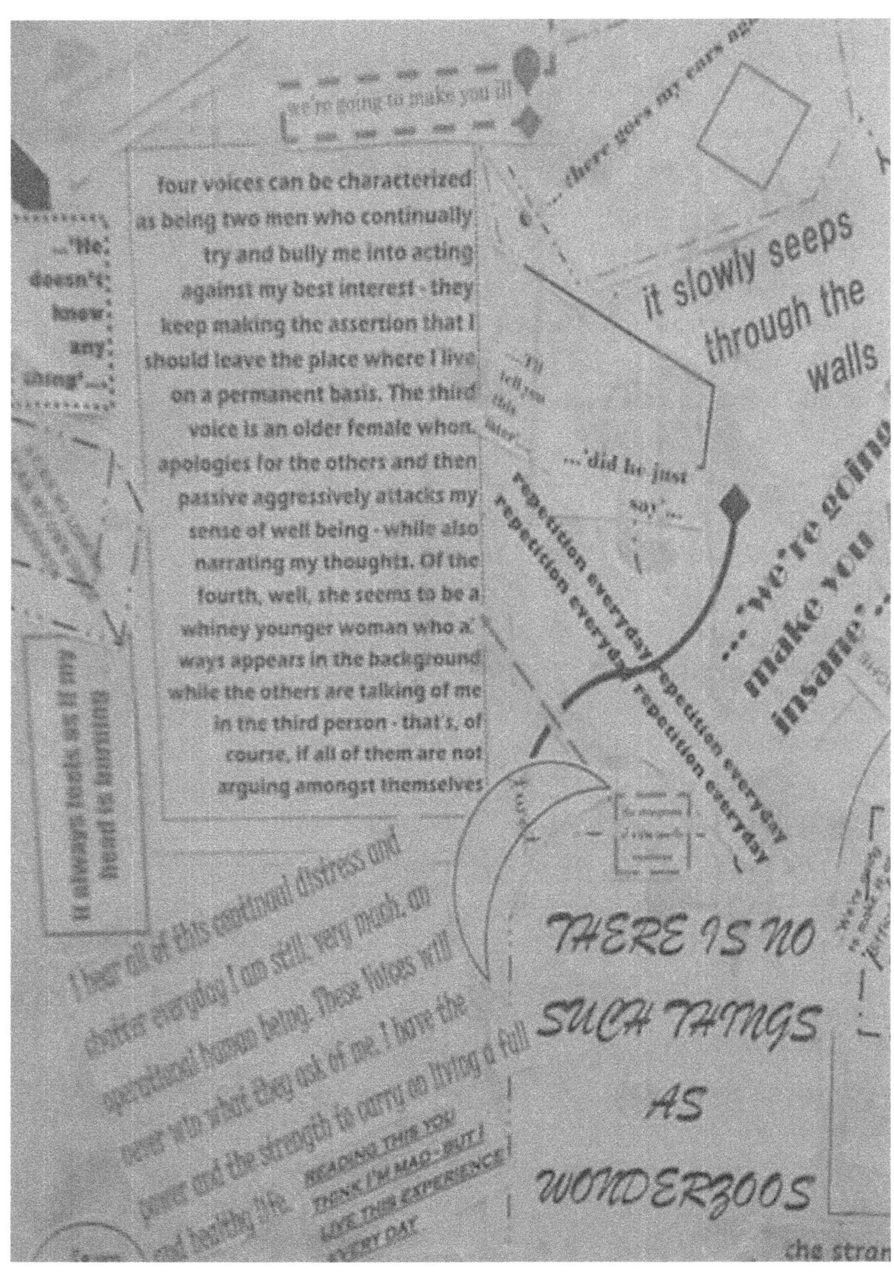
we're going to make you ill
...'He doesn't know any thing'...
four voices can be characterized as being two men who continually try and bully me into acting against my best interest - they keep making the assertion that I should leave the place where I live on a permanent basis. The third voice is an older female whom apologies for the others and then passive aggressively attacks my sense of well being - while also narrating my thoughts. Of the fourth, well, she seems to be a whiney younger woman who always appears in the background while the others are talking of me in the third person - that's, of course, if all of them are not arguing amongst themselves
it slowly seeps through the walls
...'I'll tell you this later'
...'did he just say'...
...'we're going make you insane'...
repetition everyday
repetition everyday
it always reads me if my mind is fractured
I hear all of this continual distress and chatter everyday I am still very much, an operational human being. These voices will never win what they ask of me. I have the power and the strength to carry on living a full and healthy life
READING THIS YOU THINK I'M MAD - BUT I LIVE THIS EXPERIENCE EVERY DAY
THERE IS NO SUCH THINGS AS WONDERZOOS
che stran

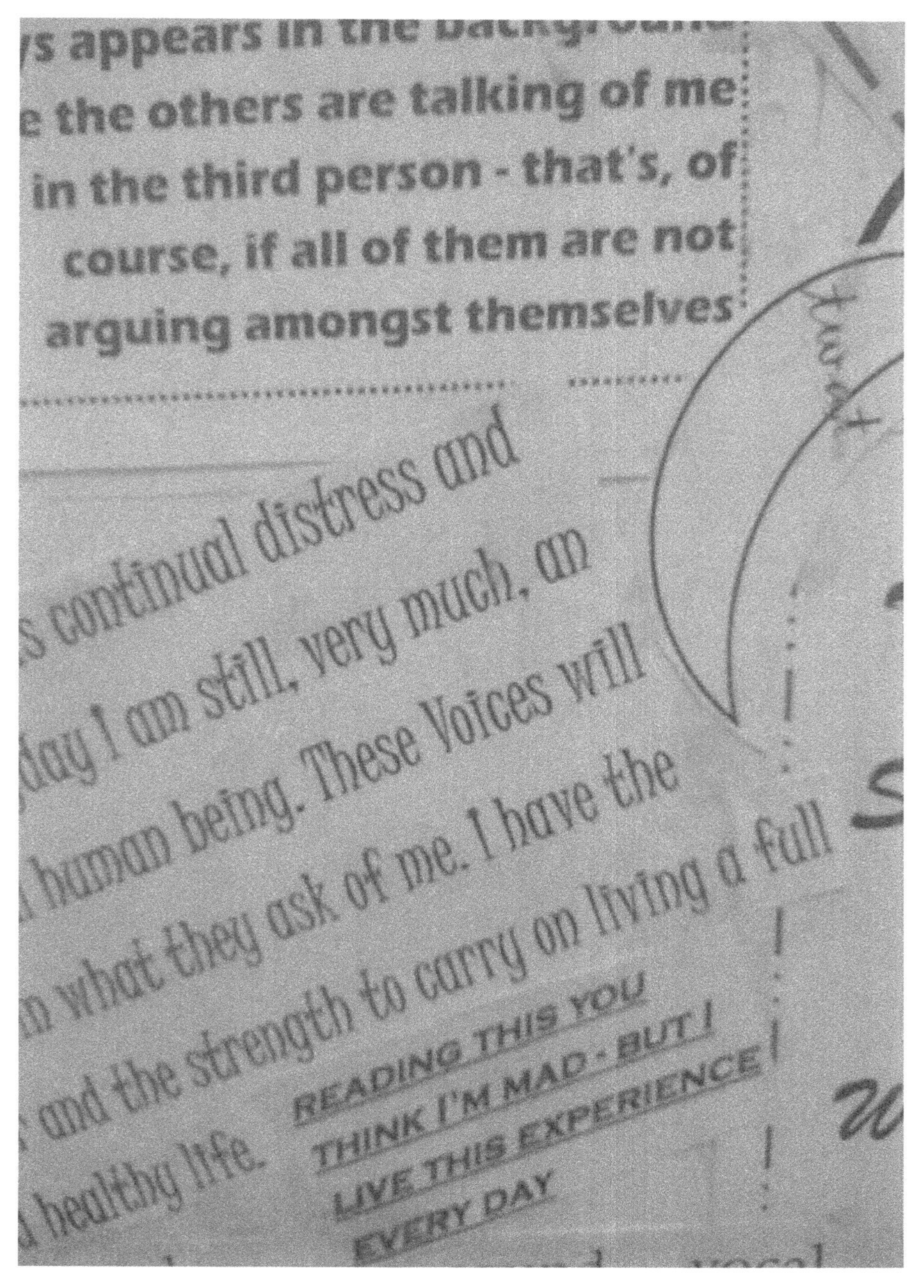
s appears in the background
e the others are talking of me
in the third person - that's, of
course, if all of them are not
arguing amongst themselves
continual distress and
day I am still, very much, an
human being. These Voices will
what they ask of me. I have the
and the strength to carry on living a full
healthy life.
READING THIS YOU
THINK I'M MAD - BUT I
LIVE THIS EXPERIENCE
EVERY DAY

hat they ask

the strength to carry on liv

thy life.

READING THIS YOU
THINK I'M MAD - BUT
LIVE THIS EXPERIEN
EVERY DAY

poly-voca   sound

speaking vocal noise

unrelenting vocal non

vocal   harassment

night vocal day vocal n

...'we're goi
...'we're
make you
insane'...
place a
same space
NWEING EARACHE /
tition everyday
tion everyday
E IS NO
'...We're going
to make it as
difficult as
possible to
omplete this
piece...'

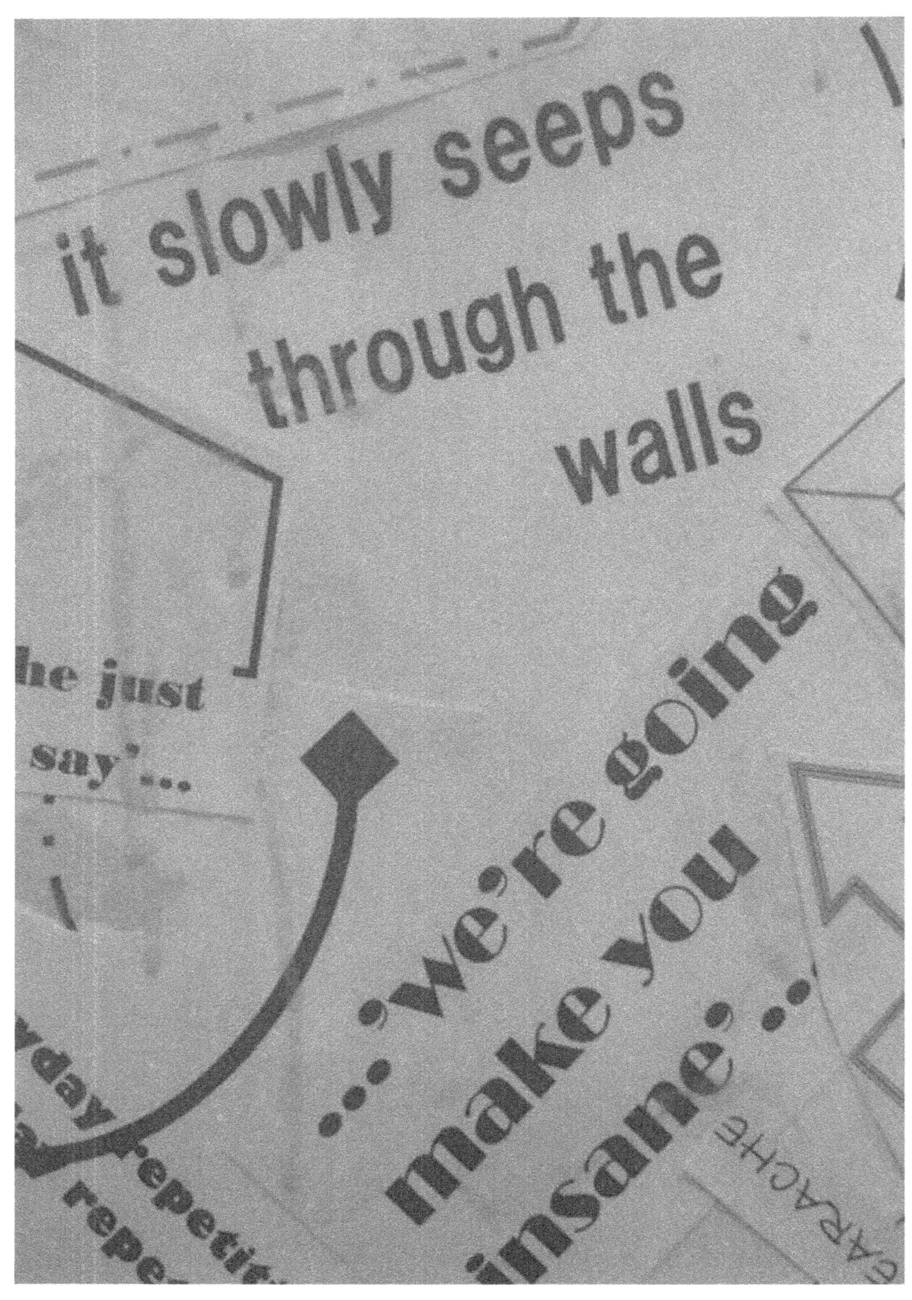
it slowly seeps
through the
walls
he just
say"...
...'we're going
make you
insane'...
we're going
day
repetit
repe

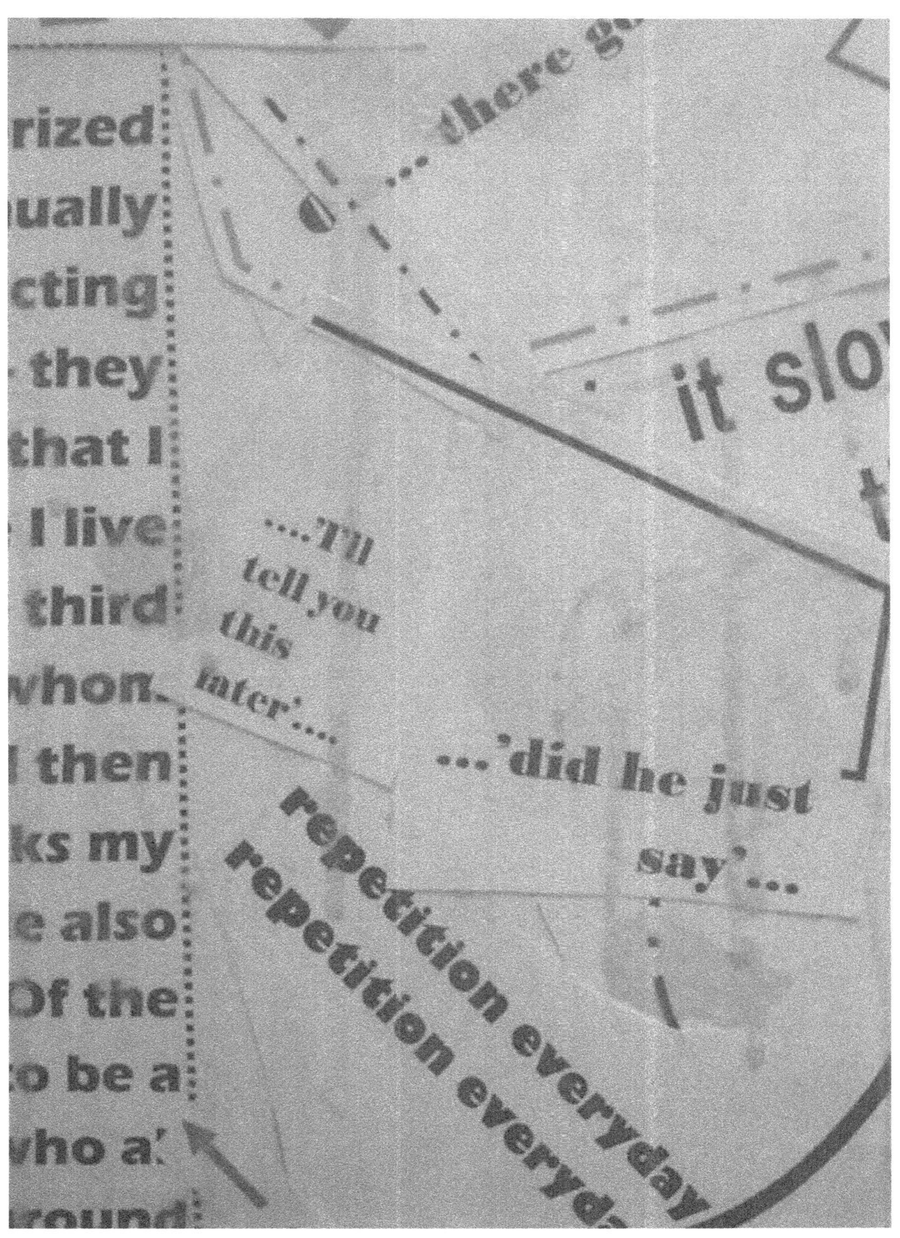
rized
ually
cting
they
that I
I live
third
whon
then
ks my
also
Of the
to be a
who a
round
... there g
... 'I'll tell you this later' ...
it slo
... 'did he just say' ...
repetition everyday
repetition everyday
repetition everyd

… **Winter Light** …

Winter light streams down the stairwell turning
the walls red through the blood hues of the curtain.
                              Life as a Venetian Carnival mask –
do you desire the everlasting sublime?
These are the dreams of my slowly descending
fall, black becoming a sublime colour;
but blue will be the warmest of them all.
                              How do I reclaim these darkened shadows?
I keep coming back to the same Pythagorean
formulas – Christ! What it feels to be alive?
Of which mode does this new improvisation
take, in which direction, of which Coltrane
change? Why should we not want all the beauty?
                              People who use the words, 'is he being
serious,' have no place in my life – Sand
in male attire. What are these flashes
of perfume? Why do I want to smell incense
smoking from a censer?
                              My soul is tethered
in winter; there is little hope of spring.
I'm feeling today a little esoteric –
I always hate to deal with someone which
neither hears or understands nothing at all.
                              January is a month of Coltrane and
Chopin, of chromatics and modes, of
different centuries reaching for hope.
How do we sing songs of a ragged age?
                              Hölderlin and Clare cross landscapes
their respective minds shucking apart in
multiplicity, as this city becomes
a mill stone around my neck, '… whenever
I tried to sing of love, it turned to pain.
And again, when I tried to sing of pain,
it turned to love.'

You know nothing about
poetry!! Ok then, write me something
in anapest trimeter, and then I'll
tell you if you know anything about
poetry?
Juan Bauza's silent missing
piano gathering dust at Valldemossa,
silence ripping through into the twenty
first century.

… Ripples …

This romanticism has become dark,
like blood dripping from the thorn of a red
red rose.
      This week I have a lost feeling
echoing through my body – it ripples
in an ocean of space. It goes without
saying, if I could, I would leave this
pessimistic city, because I
am bored with not having silence in my
life; in the place where I live, between those
brick walls. Sometimes I think this madness will
destroy me, shred me, grate me, like an ocean
grates a pebble: this now unquiet
utterance of the soul forms a new
landscape.
      These are not hazy lit neon
days. I mean what is poetry? Is it
the concrete, or is it about feeling
and sensuality? What does it mean
when you feel you can't live your life freely
and openly anymore? Once I would
have written about you: this was never
a psychedelic tango. I always
hate it when you can't get into a book
and find your intellectual way:
slowly I am turning into my own
fiction.
      There has to be more to life than
than this fucking flat white coffee: having
already lost everything I now have
nothing more to lose. This is now the new
rule, this is how I will measure myself.
It was eventually on this spring morning
when he walked out on his life: remember

I am mad, crazy, unhinged, there are more
cracks in my mental ontology, than
in the scattered broken shards of a
mirror.
            I can now, at least, think of new
possibilities, new philosophical
possibilities, I just have to live
with this final madness and these constant
gibbering noises. What is there now to say
about this life? These are the differences
between you and me: I'm unsure whether
this is, or is not a prayer? The older
I become the more esoteric my
feelings, for I am stuck in a philosophical
paradigm shift from which I can't escape.
I just want to write crazy blithering
nonsense and make you high!
                        This will always
be a new leap into the darkness as
I come to a strange, wonderous, cross
roads in life – just let yourself go mad and
live, for these are my ashes, my cinders,
this is everything burnt to dust. At this
point in my life I am no longer caged,
and refuse to be caged so – this is my
freedom, my choice. This could be a final
poem?
            You could say my thoughts were a lit-le
too kinky for this time of the afternoon!

… **1924** …

JAMES JONES

WHO AM I?

Jason was sat in his favourite armchair watching some daytime telly when there was a knock at the front door of his tiny two-up two-down, mid-terraced house. He eased himself out of his seat and made his way to the window to see if he could see who it was disturbing his afternoon off. Unable to ascertain who it was he made his way over to answer the door, to find out who it was interrupting his quiet afternoon viewing.

"Who the … can that be?" Jason mumbled to himself out loud as he slowly made his way to the door.

"Who is it?" he loudly called out through the closed door.

"Mr Pritchard?" came an enquiring female voice from the other side of the door.

"Who wants to know?" he asked, rather annoyed at being disturbed on one of his days off.

"It's Miss Bradford-Edwards," came the reply.

"What do you want? I don't want to buy anything, and I don't do visitors," he blurted out.

"Would you open the door please? I may have something of interest to you," the lady sweetly asked.

Reluctantly Jason opened the door a little to find an attractive bespectacled middle-aged woman, smartly dressed in a tweed suit standing on his doorstep.

"Whatever you're selling, I'm not interested, not in the least bit interested," he put very bluntly.

"Are you Mr Jason Pritchard?" the woman asked with a friendly smile, and kindly demeanour.

"I said, whatever you're selling, I am not interested."

He went to slam the door on her but on some vague instinct, stopped.

"I can assure you Mr Pritchard, that I am not selling anything. Would it be possible to come in for a few minutes please? I do need some information from you," she said with a smile.

"Oh, I suppose so. It's my rest day, I don't usually like to be disturbed. You'd better come in" Jason grumbled.

"Can I be cheeky and ask for a cup of tea please?" Miss Bradford-Edwards asked as she stepped into the sitting room and sat in his chair, hoping the request would calm the man down.

"Mmm," he grumbled. "Milk and sugar?"

"Just milk thank you Mr Pritchard, no sugar."

Jason gave her a look that said that's my chair, as he went into the kitchen to make the teas.

The investigator looked around at the shabby abode, thinking to herself, 'how can anyone live like this' although it was tidy enough, everything in the room looked very old and battered.

By the time Jason returned with the mugs of tea, he'd calmed down and accepted that this smartly dressed woman probably wasn't here to try and sell him anything.

"Would you like a biscuit with the tea?" he asked as he reluctantly turned the TV off.

"No, no thank you, not for me."

"Alright, now, what could be of interest to me? what is it that you want?" he asked a little more calmly.

She took out a file from her attaché case, opened it and found a pen.

"My name is, as I said, Miss Bradford-Edwards and I would like to ask you a few questions to ascertain a little about you, if that is alright with you Mr Pritchard."

"I suppose so," he replied with a loud sigh.

The female opened up her note pad, took the top off her fountain pen, ready to start taking notes.

"Firstly, can I ask you, is your name Jason Pritchard?"

"Yes, that's me, Jason Pritchard."

"Any middle names?"

"No, it's just Jason Pritchard NMI."

"Oh," a confused Miss Bradford-Edwards replied.

"No middle initial, ha-ha," Jason said with a bit of a laugh.

"I see. And will you be 49 on 17th October this year?"

"How do you know that? And – what's this all about?" he answered a little bemused.

"Just another couple of questions and I'll explain a little more. Have you lived here for, let me check, 12 years now?" she asked as she looked down at her paperwork.

"That's right, it was 12 years last month, why are you asking me all this?" his curiosity building.

"And finally, were you brought up by your grandparents after your mother died in childbirth?"

"Well, yes, as far as I can remember."

She begins to explain a little more.

"You see Mr Pritchard; I work for a company that deals with untraceable descendants."

"I don't think you'd call me 'untraceable,'" he replied.

"No, not in the first instance. However, sometimes there are individuals whose past is not all they believe it to be. My job is to track down males of your age named Jason Pritchard."

"I'll bet there's plenty of them," he said with a grin on his face.

"You wouldn't believe how many, you are my seventeenth so far. Now, I wonder if you could tell me about your life, with as much detail as you can remember?" she asked as she sat with pen and paper at the ready.

Jason thought for a little while, took a sip of his tea while trying his best to recall his early years.

"Well, as you rightly said, I was brought up by my grandparents, in a tied cottage on a, I think it was a farm, quite a big farm from what I can recall. But I didn't know my mother had died in childbirth until I was about eight or nine, they kept that from me. So I never knew my real mother. And they never told me who my father was, and I still don't know who he is to this day. I suppose he must be dead by now as well."

Looking up from her notepad, she picked up her tea, took a sip then she asked, "what do you remember about your education?"

"My Uncle Reg used to take me to the local school, I think it must have been about a mile or so away, he used to take me on his bike, with me on the cross bar. He did that until he met a girl and got married. My other uncle, Uncle Bert, used to come and pick me up from school, but he met a girl and got married, leaving me to live with Nan and Grandad."

"And can you remember what your grandparents did for a living?"

"I think my Grandad worked on the farm and my Nan cleaned in the big house where the farmer and his wife lived with their strange son, well, my uncles thought he was strange."

"Now that is interesting. What about when you left school, you joined the army did you not?"

"Yes, but that was more to do with my grandparents, they were getting old and looking after me and working on the farm started to become too much for them. Not only that, but the cottage was needed for new workers for the farm. I'd seen the posters for the Army, so decided to join up. I can still remember my Nan's cooking though, the tantalising smells and tastes that she created, so the catering corps seemed to me the place to be," Jason recalled with a little softness in his voice.

"So you will receive a bit of a pension from the army in due course I presume."

"Yes, but it won't amount to much, I only served up to the age of 28. That's when I met my wife, Angela. We had plans to settle down and start a family of our own but, unfortunately, that never happened."

Miss Bradford-Edwards made a few more notes before looking up to Jason and asking, "Can I ask why that was?"

"It's not important now, but with my HGV licence that I gained while in the army, I started lorry driving for Hugo Haulage, I still work there as it happens. But they put me through for a class 'one' licence in order to do long-distance haulage, you know, continental trips. Angela wasn't happy with that because I was away a lot. She had an affair with some bloke, we broke up and eventually got divorced."

"Are you in a relationship now Mr Pritchard?"

He looked up at her, half wondering if he should tell her.

"It doesn't have any bearing on anything I am looking into, it's just for my information," Miss Bradford-Edwards explained.

"Well," he hesitated, took another sip of his tea, "I am living with, or should I say she is living here with me from time to time. Her name is Shelagh, Shelagh Wagstaff. Shelagh works in the office for Hugo Haulage, she's almost part of the fixtures there."

"So she doesn't live here with you all the time then?" she asked.

"No, she has a flat in town. Sometimes she stays here, sometimes I go to her flat and sometimes we have some time to ourselves. Seems to work okay."

"Does Shelagh have any children?"

"No, no, neither of us have any children. Shelagh is an only child, like me. So we have no-one else to answer to. It actually suits us both quite nicely," Jason added with a bit of a glint in his eye.

Miss Bradford-Edwards took another sip of her tea, set the cup down and made more notes on her pad.

"And Miss Wagstaff …"

"Mrs. Shelagh was married, but that didn't work out. Apparently he played the field, as they say. Shelagh wasn't having any of that, so they separated. Her divorce will be, what do they call it? Absolute, any day soon."

Miss Bradford-Edwards made a few more notes, picked up the cup and finished her tea.

"This is purely curiosity on my part, and I'll not be making a note of it but do you both intend to get married? It's just my personal interest, I do see a great many situations like yours and, as I said, I'm just curious."

"We have talked about it, and it could be a possibility, but I'll leave the final decision to Shelagh. She's better at making those sorts of choices than me."

"Well Mr Pritchard, that will be all for the time being, except for one more tiny detail."

"Right, and what is that then?"

"Would you mind if I took a swab for DNA tests?" she asked as she took a small test kit out of her attaché case.

Rather taken aback at this strange request, Jason hesitated. "I'm not sure. Why would you want to check my DNA?"

"It will enable us to confirm, or otherwise, whether or not we should continue along the path we have to take, with the information you have given me today, Mr Pritchard," she explained.

"Okay, I suppose it's alright," he reluctantly agreed.

Miss Bradford-Edwards took a swab from his mouth, placed the stick into a tube and then proceeded to pack all her things away.

"We should have the results by early next week. Would it be alright to call on you again, shall we say on Thursday, at about four in the afternoon?"

"Let me just check my rota for next week," Jason got up to look at the calendar to see what his duties were. "Actually, I'm working away Tuesday to Thursday, but Friday I'll be here, so will Shelagh as it happens."

"Shall we say next Friday at four in the afternoon then?"

"Yes, right, I'll write it on my calendar."

Miss Bradford-Edwards made a note of the appointment in her diary and bid Jason a good afternoon.

The Following Friday

Jason and Shelagh were sitting in the front room, Shelagh looked at the Clock, it was five minutes to four.

"Five to four Jas," Shelagh pointed out.

"Yes, I see, five to four."

"That lady should be here very soon Jas, have you any idea what it could all be about? I know you said she wanted to know all about you, but why I wonder," Shelagh pondered.

"I really have no idea. Although she did say she might have 'something of interest' to me, when I opened the door to her last week."

There was a knock at the door. Jason got up to answer it. Both he and Shelagh had tried to make the place a little more presentable, as well as dressing up a bit.

Jason ushered Miss Bradford-Edwards into the sitting room where she immediately sat in Jason's chair.

"Hello, I'm Shelagh, Miss …"

"Bradford-Edwards, but please call me Clementine, that's teen as in teenager. And you must be Mrs Wagstaff, I'm very pleased to meet you."

"Like wise, Clementine, and please call me Shelagh. Would you like a cup of tea?"

"That would be lovely. Milk, no sugar thank you."

Shelagh went to the kitchen to make the tea while Jason perched on the sofa, opposite Miss Bradford-Edwards.

"So, Jason, can I call you Jason?"

"That's fine Miss Bradford-Edwards, Jason will be fine."

"Please call me Clementine, Jason. May I ask about your week? Have you thought anymore about the questions I asked?"

"Well, Miss Brad, er Clementine, I have gone over it a few times with Shelagh, but I can't think of anything else at all. I think I've told you everything I can remember," he replied.

Clementine opened her attaché case and took out a file, the file appeared to be much thicker than Jason remembered her having the week previously. Opening the file, she removed a few pages from it and placed them on the floor in front of her. Meanwhile, Shelagh returned with the teas.

"Let me clear the coffee table for you Clementine, you can put your papers on it. One tea, milk with no sugar, I'll get the biscuits," said Shelagh.

"Not for me, thank you Shelagh. The tea will be just fine."

Shelagh handed Jason his tea and sat down beside him on the threadbare sofa. Clementine sorted the papers out, took a sip of tea, then picked up the first page.

"You both work for Hugo Haulage, is that correct?" Clementine asked.

"Yes, that's right. I've actually been there for, oh, it must be twenty plus years. I take care of the office work, organising the drivers and their jobs, as well as ordering diesel, overseeing the maintenance programme and, of course, the wages. They really moan if I don't get it right. I usually do, but now and then I make the odd wrong calculation, they soon let me know," Shelagh laughingly informed her.

"A lot of responsibility then," Clementine replied.

"It's a job. Most of the time it works quite smoothly. It's only occasionally we get tiresome hiccups. But they're usually sorted without too many problems."

"So, down to business, we had you're DNA results back on Tuesday, with what appear to be very positive results," Clementine informed them.

Jason gazed at Clementine, not too sure what that all meant.

"Is that good or bad?" he asked.

"As far as I'm concerned, for you it would seem to be good, very good. However, we do need to clarify one or two things."

Shelagh looked at Jason, who didn't seem to be able to understand what that meant.

"Please Clementine, can you enlighten us?" Shelagh asked.

"Well, about a year ago, the farm, or should I say the manor house and estate, where you were born and raised Jason, became vacant due to the death of the son. I believe your uncles called him 'strange'."

"Yes, that's right," Jason agreed with a chuckle.

"The son, Tarquin Brendon Hugo-Jones, was the only descendant of his parents, or so it was believed. You see, Tarquin was gay so never married and therefore never had any children to leave the estate to. When he died, just over a year ago, my office was called in to investigate the situation. When we did a search of the house, several documents were uncovered that proved of great interest," Clementine explained.

"I'm not sure I understand, or what it has to do with me," a confused Jason uttered.

"Just bear with me please Jason. Tarquin's mother had kept detailed diaries with information about Brendon Hugo-Jones, her husband, and his philandering. She also kept details of several lovers she herself had. There is absolutely no evidence of any of these relationships resulting in any other children – except one. Are you with me so far?"

Shelagh spoke for a confused Jason.

"Are you saying what I think you're saying?"

"I do believe that you Shelagh, have picked up on the unconfirmed at this stage, probability of the results of our investigation. In fact, my colleagues back in the office are awaiting a call at this moment with the final answer. As soon as they get it, they will call me and inform me of the outcome."

Shelagh took a hold of Jason's hand with her trembling hand.

"You're trembling my love, why?" Jason asked.

"I think this could possibly be something big, very big, darling," Shelagh replied with a little tremble in her voice.

Clementine smiled as she looked at the couple as they held one another.

"You're right, Shelagh. It is starting look that way. You see, Lord Brendon Hugo-Jones, started up a haulage company, in partnership with a local businessman."

"Excuse me, Clementine, did you say 'Lord'?" a bewildered Shelagh asked.

"That is correct. Hugo-Jones remained a 'silent partner' leaving the running of the business 'Hugo Haulage' to the businessman." Clementine explained.

"Our Hugo Haulage?" Jason asked.

"Yes, Hugo Haulage where you are both employed. The estate of Hugo-Jones has a forty-nine percent interest in the company, currently valued at approximately £2.5 million pounds. That figure is just an estimate at this time. The important item to bear in mind for you, Jason, is, how do I put it, well, you know who your mother is, but not your father," Clementine added.

"That's right Miss, er, Clementine. There is no record, as far as I know, of who he was." Jason clarified.

"Well Jason, I do believe that is about to change." A mobile phone rang, Clementine picked it up to answer it. "Excuse me for a moment. I'll just step outside to take this call."

"You can go into the kitchen if that would be easier for you," Shelagh offered.

"Thank you, I will."

Miss Bradford-Edwards made her way into the kitchen to take the call, shutting the door behind her.

"This is all very strange, strange and intriguing. I wonder what the phone call is about?" Shelagh said, rather nervously.

"I'm not at all sure that I can grasp all this, it's weird, don't you think?" Jason added.

"Yes, my Lord."

"Don't be silly, there's more chance of us winning the lottery than me being a Lord. And we don't know what Clementine's call is about, it may prove to be nothing, nothing at all. I'll bet that I'm not even the Jason Pritchard that she's looking for," a nervous Jason said.

"I think everything is pointing to her investigations, to find the right person, is about to end here and now, or very soon at least," Shelagh said with an upbeat and positive inclination. "She did say she was waiting for a call from her colleague in the office."

Miss Bradford-Edwards came back into the living room with a huge smile on her face. She sat back in Jason's chair, picked up the papers, made a couple of notes on her pad, looked up at Jason and Shelagh, still smiling.

"Well, Jason Pritchard, I have just been informed that our investigations into the Hugo-Jones estate, have, at last, come to a conclusion. That was my colleague in the office, and I can now confirm that you, Jason, once the appropriate forms have all been signed and witnessed, are about to become quite wealthy," Miss Bradford-Edwards stated.

"What? what do you mean? How can this be at all possible? These things don't happen to the likes of me." Jason managed to garble.

"Can you explain please? Can you enlighten us?" Shelagh asked.

"Certainly. After thorough, very thorough investigations, and with the information gleaned from the diaries and papers of Lady Cynthia Hugo-Jones, along with unmistakable DNA results, you, Jason Pritchard have inherited the Manor house, the entire estate and a forty-nine percent share of Hugo Haulage."

"Don't you mean Lord Jason, Clementine?" Shelagh pointed out.

"I'm afraid that at this time, we cannot verify that the title will pass to Jason. It has to go through the official channels which are overseen by the Royal household. That isn't to say that, eventually, it may pass to you, but we will have to wait until it has passed through their hands. It may be that your personal details have to be altered and your name changed to Hugo-Jones, as Lord Brendon Hugo-Jones is, without any doubt, your natural, biological father," Clementine proudly announced.

Jason sat there, utterly gobsmacked. Speechless and almost traumatised.

Shelagh spoke for him, "Is this a big, I mean a life changing situation for us? I mean for Jason?"

"The Manor house and all the land, which is approximately 50 hectares, has an estimated value of £12 million pounds. That figure is unsubstantiated, it could easily be worth much more. When the final figures are calculated my colleague in the office, has estimated that you, Jason Pritchard, will be worth between £14 and £16 million, that is the approximation of my colleague."

"What would I do with all that? Surly that can't be all mine. I just wouldn't know where to start," an astonished Jason interjected.

"I should point out that those figures only relate to the property and business assets," Miss Bradford-Edwards added.

Shelagh looked at Jason and then at Clementine, "You mean there's more?"

"Yes, indeed there is more. There are some savings accounts and investments that Tarquin held. They are currently yielding returns of £150,000 per annum. Tarquin was a shrewd man when it came to financial matters."

"Why that's, let me see, more than four times more than our joint income now," Shelagh calculated.

"It is my duty to advise you to take legal advice on all these aspects of our findings. We do have a very good solicitor who deals with this type of case, and I suggest you get in touch first thing Monday morning. I will call his secretary to let her know that you will be calling, and I am sure he will be more than happy to carry out any and all aspects of the searches, legalities and associated works involved," Clementine advised.

"So can we take it that we, or rather Jason, has inherited all of this, absolutely no doubt whatsoever?" Shelagh asked.

"Absolutely, Shelagh, one hundred percent. No doubt at all. Right, that's my job done, and I'd like to offer my congratulations Jason. Here is a letter, from me, outlining everything for you, including our companies details along with our approximations. Enjoy your newfound wealth and may I wish you both every happiness for your future together. I'll just quickly call our solicitors PA and I'll be gone."

Miss Bradford-Edwards made the call, picked up the papers, tucked them into her attaché case and left Jason and Shelagh to take in what had just unfolded.

Jason threw his arms around Shelagh, they hugged and kissed, and screamed with delight.

"Has all this just happened? I mean *really* happened?" Jason asked.

"Here's the letter Clementine has left for you, outlining everything. Look, the letterhead proves that all this is legitimate, no question, it's for real."

They screamed with delight again.

"Let's have a Chinese and a bottle of wine to celebrate," an elated Jason suggested.

They both screamed with delight again as they danced around the dowdy living room.

MERRIS LONGSTAFF

POEMS FROM A SOBER WITNESS

Covantry Calling

Mi memba ear de anounsar warn
Disa de final call fi all passenga leavin on de 07.30 trian fi goa Covantry
Mi stanup, not evan sure ifa mi shi mean
So widout entire convictian, at dat time
Mi jump on de train at 07. 29
So, how mi get ear …

De firs day af twenty twenty two
Mi get notice seh mi afi go somewear
Immedately
Mi ear anadda jurney await fi mi
An ita go start afta mi walk tru de terminal giate
Mi no evan get chance fi pack praperly
Or tell anybady mi gaan
But more alarmin was
De speed at wich mi associate dem exit de departure loung
It genarate wan piece a vacuum yu si
So forceful, cole ear chill mi, an it reek af finality
Recoverin fram dat tialspin, mi look roun, an no si nobady mi kno
Is only den mi realize
Mi afi mek de jorney
To Covantry
Alone

Mi cyaan lie an say mi neva tink de sitiation ago happm
Caus a few times, mi fine miself astudy de attitude
Of soma de people roun mi
It feel like one or two adem waan eek out any visible shard af mi
brokeness

Jus so dem cyan jook me agen, an agen an agen
An yet most, like angels hole mi up
How else mi cudda stay dear fi ova four ears?
Four ears alang time man
Mia wanda if mi did stay too lang
 Despite de sudden nature of di call fi move
Mi kno seh, mia go dear fi get new experience
Yu si, mi nat a real stranga a Covantry
Mi send dear aready, afta de odda crowd mi did wit, kick mi out
Mi seh, adat force isolaton nearly kill mi
But is only bare courige mek mi crawl out dat hole
An against all adds emerge sublime
But only to deflate rapidly
Ina disya worl dat still cyaant comfort or tether me!

Now, wit wan way ticket ina mi han
Mi kno mi naa com back
An on tap, mi sens mi powarless fi push weh
De vice af de bein
No mortal eva seein
Dearfore, bline and wit only fait as currancy
Mi go afi patient and si how evryting ago unfole
In de meantime, mia look farward fi alikkle space, peace an time
Fi sidung an clearout mi head
Mi no do dat exarcise fi ovar five ears now
An aredy de cansquence ashow
Mi stagnant
An mus plead guilty to starvin an ignore mi inna chile
Whils always agorge de outar man
Wat a sin
Mi gaan

Meghan Markle Matters

Evry woman matta
Dat a fac evry right tinkin person kno
Howeva, sometimes, ano so it go
Mi si plenty a evidence
Sho many pride dem cola above odda
An believe seh, aonly white race matta

Yes dem deserve de bes af evryting
An dem cyaan standby an watch
Any adda cola even try fi get a slice ar win
Especially when shia black

A Meghan Markle mia talk bout!
De woman accomplish in shi own right
Yet all kina message sen out sey
Ina in disa lan, compear wit white
Megan undeservin of any lite
Especially when it com to de fina tings in life.

Dees haytas love fi invade, shame an insis shi keep anda par
Why, why di war?
Mi sey, is because one drap a black blood ina har

Now, non adem so fool fi stanup alone
An call owt har stain loud
Instead, evrywear dem farm big crowd
An anda cova, serve up di gyal
Big pliates of all tings negative
Well season in de dirt of white privilidge

 Mi seh de gyal cyaan do right fi doin wrang
Tek how shi choose har flowas fi har weddin day
A ting all brides like fi dem way
Megan no get credit fi har beautiful spray

Instead, dem report seh har bouquet did dangarous
An put at risk, princess Charlotte
Shi a likkle white chile wit approve white royal status

Now mia go soun like a bitch
But mia afi seh, if di sitiation did switch
Ana Meghan chile did ave allargy, nobady wud even kno bout it
Or even give ashit

So u si, Meghan charge wit sin evan before har weddin
An becaus shi no trow weh har good good ting
Fi fully accamadate Charlotte sensitivity
De story dem mek so ugly
Unu wuda tink Meghan a Myra Hindley

Dem cyant put Meghan behine bars
So frustrate, de zealots fixiate an demanizing har
Wi ear, Meghan consumptian of advocado pears
Link to poor practice ina som cantinent
Ana caus drouts, human right abuse an destructian of envirinment
Yu no si? widout trial
Meghan bran a pariah

Now Kiate no subjec to all dis side yiy and judgement
Wen shi did prignant
Shi like fi gush about dis syame supa food
Mi no ear any ado
Mi seh nat one eyebrow raise
Shi get praise
Meghan repriman

Now what wi shud call all dis kinda ting?
Som seh a nutn, and black woman too sensitive
Mi seh, dees scoundrels always deny an try fi hide
But adem relentless negativity
Dat best showcase dem bigatry
Dem drive is always partray Meghan
As less dan.

My Friend Joy

Of all de nyame ina de worl fi give gyal pickney
Har madda choose fi call de miggle one of har brood, Joy
Joy u know! Mi imagine ita de experience of great pleasha
Mose maddas feel wen dem look pan new barn byabe

Howeva, to dis day, Ann reason fi call shi daughta Joy
Still no clear
Far it look like, rada dan sinting good
Joy's purpose in life did beset wit all kinda abstacle
Misandastood, dem slowly fashian har as a containa
Dat mus keep fullup to de brim
An many times ovaflowin unda de weight of har madda aganies
An de tartment of som siblin rivalry

Mi aftin wanda if christening har daughta, Joy
Did actually root ina visian har madda get
Dat, like a degeh seed, Joy ago gro an com to bless de family
Unda de rite conditians dat cuda well ahappm
But, evan now it seem Joy purpose no realize ina dat enviriment
Dem judge her fruit too bitta
Mi always a ask miself
Why

Perhaps mi bias, for mi kno Joy a lang time an mia get to kno har well
Shi divine, warm, compassioniate an a seeka of souls,
But har mout nuh license by any church
Har energy did too bright fi soma de family, so dem tek dem time an
whip har dry
Skillfully tamparin wit har greatest fear in life
Abandanment.
Anyway, afta what seemed a lifetime af punishment
Joy wake up wan day, tell harself har trute an walk weh

Mi swear, adat process help define har, evan tiday,
Har courige to walk weh fram fidem prison gate
Lead Joy to seek har own light, and absorb the pasitive energy of
odders in flight.
Sure, shi mek a few mistyake, an plenty plenty time mi si shi fall flat an
har fyace
Only to ressurec, an transfarm har brokeness into a special gif fi adders
Humility
Mi jus love watchin the many ways shi grow ova de ears
Paradoxically, har absence may very well tun roun and bless de family
Far now, Joy aglow wit age, and afta all, widout har, dema only rejectin
de conditians weer true healin begin
Rite now data fi dem lass, far mi certain, mi frien nuh call Joy fi notn

New Age Niggers

Nigger a nyame people create fi call black man
It startup lang time now, but it did ave real impact.
Dere was no odder who coulda challenge or argue wit dat one super powa
De caucasian man, who wit bible an gun
Only seek to stap nigger hart and drain dem brain
Yes sah, blacks were emptied, and called to worship
Those who yeil jus manage fi stay alive, as did their chilren
An dear chilren children …
Man, a hole heap a generation adem.

Nobady did si we trial
Black man afi lay down lo
Som evan gwaan like dem dead
An still odders jus survive but only fi languish ina exile
For unda rule of white supremacy
Black man, nigga no count like dema smadi

So, white man mek almighty woun ina worl
An to dis day, dat rent still prominent
Anyway, today mia afi seh tank Gad for greata is de pull
Fi remove negativity and pudung all weapans dat prove dull
Wite supremacy is only one, but it afi, afi afi go
Why?
De minority world say so.
Now dema get sense
An beside dem, unu look ugly, dungrow and dense

Afta all, unu no si
Wedday America elec an put black man ina wite house
Dat go against all wite supremacy policy
As well, dactor perfarm tousands af operatian on dead people, and fine proof seh
No care how wi look
Ander de skin wi no diffran
Dem evan write it ina medical book

 Still, in de fyace of de ovawhelmin evidence dat wi all equal
Dear exist a few who disya worl cyant break, shake or make accept or
anastan
Wi all belang to de family of man, ana dem w_ afi respec and serve
White supremacists listen
Unu status well ago run dry
An soon unu ago fine unuself at the battam of the pile
Perhaps den unu will tek de time
To go figar, is who a nigga?

Portrait of me

Las week mi sidung alook tru ole photograf
A whol eap adem,
Som mi neva look pan in ova 50 ears
An soma di peeple, mi no evan memba dem nyame.
Is nearly a hole day me spen an it,
But is only when mi nearly don
Mi fine a likkle one a me
Mi musi about a four ears ole pickney
Wen mi did live ina Jamaica wit mi aunty dem

What a find!
Mi aunty fix mi hear good u si, and mi pink dress did cute
But fia alang time, all mi cud do is look ina mi yiy dem
Disya feature really disturb mi mood
Caus deep in mi yiy mi si a likkle chile alone
Troubled an nat evan a likkle frisky!
Unu cyaan si? mi yiy dem experienced.
Mia steer direc ina de cyamra
An wit de air of a seer, convey mi did awear some serias shit ago down
and mi afi well prepear

Mi neva kno it, but at de time dis piccha was de afficial key fi coma Englan
An all mi cyan say is, ita good job mi did briace myself.
Englan was nat like de playgroun mi did use to
Like, afta di magic af touchin sunow di first time, mia look roun fi sun ana likkle lite
Mi no si none!
An man, de place cole u si.
Cole, cole like mi no know what
An, an tap a dat, mi dida wanda, wid all dis stone a groun, how mia go ear when mango drap.

Lata, mi realize mi enta anada worl, wit no mango trees, an no
anastandin of how mi fit in
Strangers became mi caretakers, an ina di official playgroun a skool,
Mi learn mi diffran. Nat a difran person, but a diffran cola. an it bad
De wider worl no accep mi eida, far even afta mi lef skool, mi neva
wance, an TV, news piaper or magazine si any piccha af any black girl ar
woman in a positive lite.
No sah, Dem did always portray as sliave, dirt poor or jusa walk aroun
wit dem titty outa door

All af mi teenage ears an merge into womanhood a syame
Mi spen too lang fightin de curse af de stereyotype Englan plant ina mi
Di syame battle agwan to dis dyay
Today, mi yiy dem remine mi seh, mi did start owt lonely, so mi nat
really surprise mi com fi like mi own company
Okay, mi no live ina de bes part af de garden.
An due to insecurities mi buy, an de numerous wounds to mi pride
Mi develop plenty spikes fi protect miself
Mi spike not visible to niaked yiy, but if any a unu come too close wit
unu bullshit unu afi real careful
Far widout warnin mi cud jook you
What else cyan tharns do?

Secrets of the Windrush

All now, it ard fi tink bout
Dose crimes of life, di struggle an strife
Dat rab mi of mi lite, fite an mite

Mi memba plenty bad feelins
Evan doe, at the time
Mi was jus a likkle pickney
Ataddle aroun in nutn but a baggy

Mi seh mi feelins did wida dan any ocean
An bury down deepa dan de seas
Pan which de Windrush roar
As mi grow, mi ear seh
Wen mi madda lef
Shi cry an cry, ug an kiss mi goodbye
Now tell mi, wat in dat story cyan pacify
A canfuse chile
Hard like stone an alone?

Har disappearance change up my worl
Like, fi de firs time, mi did fraid
Fear yu kno, angry, disorient, lass, sad
An a hole heap more mi cuda add

Mi did ovawelm fi sure
An always abubble ova wit pressure
Alone, mi learn fi suppress pain
Nutn to gain
An, is no joke
From de start
Nobady notice likkle me
Adrown ina de fanfear of dat magnificent boat

So, mi an mi madda meet up ova 5 ears lata
Shi kno me, but afta so many years,
No idea of madda ina fi mi head
Almose like shi did dead
Mi madda claim mi
Wit tears in har yiy dem
An a look on har face
Mi lata fine out mean happy
Sadly it was dat invasion dat set de scene
Fi decades of misary

Most prominent, was the unspoken rule
No negative feelins mus show in disya house
Mi did always afi mek sure
Nutn ina mi mine suddenly slip, an come owt mi mout
Mi did only a chile, so it com tricky
An each time mi slip
Mi get a nip
An wat mi do was neva fargotten ar fargiven.
Likkle did dey kno, dem was craftin a scapegoat
Crippled, an foreva curse to dance
In the flames of mama trauma drama.

It's been hell,
Shhh, don't tell

The History of We

Mek mi tel unu someting
Yu si disya skin
No lite ina it.
Brown, rich, dark an full a melanin.

Dem call we black,
And som a dem people no like us
Jus because
Dem si we color look like the dirt anda dem foot

But sia
A de same mistyake mek dem march ina fi wi lan, Africa
Wit plan fi tek ova
Dem com tell we bout Jesus, dem god, de devil and sin
An wen we umble,
Dem tip toe an tife weh we good good ting
Ana store it up fi give dem queen and kings.

What a trial, mi Gad!
But like dat no nuff
Dear is even more fuckery in we history
Afta dem si wi natural bady bil good
Weder proof an strang like lion
Dem dream seh we a animal
Ripe fi laba on fidem plantation

Righteous wepan did mek wi easy prey
And wedout mercy dem conka an slay
What we cuda do?
We neva ave nutn.
So, from dat day
We impotence gave birt to de cyancer,
Negro slave
Only have wort pickin dem cotton

Yes sah!
Dem foot walk all over fi wi groun
An all di wile we no mek no soun
Becase we know, deep down
Groun a place fram where every dam ting grow
An after the cycle,
The bury an even de burn
Is destin to return

So unu si
Likkle magic ina we black
But still dem talk bout we
Lika som ting wia lack
We no lack a dam ting
Only equal, mi seh equal appatunity
To born, trive and die
Like we is yuman bein
An, we want we dimonds back

Ear mi now
What did sweet dem ova ina Africa
Soon ago sour dem
Far dem false lite ago dim
It really did only powa wit sin
And when dem ina dark
Dema go worry an friten of how tings ago run,
Wen we get fi express we full freedam
Well ova time dema go afi learn
No lite can naturally shine widout de dark
Dat is de time
Dema go si we spark.

The Music in Me

You kno one ting mi cyan stan
Wen people no treat mi like mia yuman
Okay, so sometime mi shuffle an cyaan walk good
An pain cyan lick my bady
Like only a bitch could.

Dem call mi disable
An wit dat label, com rule mi afi abserve
Like mi mus neva show mi brain cyan function
An mi cyant show mi ave a soul
Dat is entirely ander my cantrol
Some no like it.
A musa Gad give dem atarity
Fi com undamine fi mi dignity.

Mek mi tell unu wat mia talk bout
Wedday mi dress up agoa work Christmas party
De food did fine, but afta wi nyam don
Evry bady jus siddung
Talkin, lookin aroun, sipping G&T ana nack back wine.

Mi disable, but mi oil up aready
An jusa wait fi mi lova
Fi com ina de room an tek mi ova
Mi seh wen dat music com ina mi ears, an mi feel de beat
Mi jump up quick an start dance
Wit no sense af bein unsteady pan mi feet
Yes sah, de music pull mi ina trance
Si mi ya, si mi ya, si mi ya (dancing)
Ha ha ha ha ha ha

Well, de day afta
Woman com up to mi ana talk seh
How dem all surprise how well mi did move an dance floor las nite
Dat mean dema look pan mi ana judge
Wat a fuckin liberty
Man de ting shame mi yu si, shame shame
But why mi afi blame fi dem ignorance
Unu eva ear law mek fi dance?

Now wen people com angle mi wit dem kitten paws
It cyan mek mi bad like yaws
Afta all, mi no do no cyan cyan
Mi no do limbo
All mi do is jus yeil to de spirit of disco

Fi mi disabilty musa mek som people canfuse
Mi no kno why, caus ita pure lagic
Music belang ina spiritual realm
An wen absarb, cyan promote movement dat almost seamless
All dees ting breed new life ina mi disable bady
An whilst mi cyan breed
Mi nat jusa ago siddung
Nar woud I eva bow to thee

Climate Change

Wen mi was a pikney,
Sumall, way down yas so.
Mi anti tell mi seh
Rock stone a riva bottom no kno how sun hat
At de time, all mi did alook fa
Was a likkle somting fi eat
Shi no giv mi nutn
Har belief dat mi no kno bout hunga an hard ship
Did noting to cure mi cravin.
Mi still abeg har fi bread

Now mia big woman
An mi oftin tink bout de stones ina riva bottam
Ana wanda who give ordar fi dem protect from the harsh wedda
Mik cyant canclude, but gradualy mia com fi believe seh
It musa jus design af niatur,
And like dose stones
We umans, also ave owa plyace ina de universe

Now, everybady know uman diffran fram rockstone
Like, wi cyan talk, walk, tink an feel
Or so mi believe
Howeva, disa fac aturn out a dangeros cambination
Far it look like owa free will, an drive, alead us to disrespec disya worl
wia liv in

Now, let me tell unu somting,
Niatur hav boundary man cyant tampa wit
An it won't suffa insult fi lang
Dearfore it mek sense to treat any likkle evidence af sickness
Before, malignancy set in
An det inevitable
Is abuse mia talk bout
Eart abuse, it agwan fia lang tme now,
An yet, mi kno plenty people atalk seh, isa hoax
All mi cyan say is demdeh peeple musi ded,
But dem yiy no shet

Afta all, who?
Who cyant si de billowin tears di eart a shed
In the guise of rain, ita lash out har agony in contry
Wear torrent of rain wata acom like stranga
An like a tief in de nite,
It tek weh house, cyar, lan and all futur plan

While dis a gwaan
Elsewear, an in many rejons
Owa planet a decyay wit feva
Mi seh soma di place hat yu si
So hat, feva cyan jus spike ina ragin flame
An nyam out everyting in it way
Man cyan put out soma di flames
But de feva always remain
Alook fi appartunity fi creep up an bus owt again

Yes sah!
Wia also awitness feva acaus prolang an widespred drout
Mainly in country dat mose need wata fi grow dem food
Widout,
Dem afi beg, or suck salt tru wooden spoon
A true!

Even some of di worl dat did extra cole a perish
Is mainly animal a live ina dose quartas
Mi ear ova 5 and a half tousand specis in de Artic alone
Once, dis place did cova wit sunow an tick tick ice,
An now de enemy a come fi styay
Ita destroy the envirinment naitur originally gift dem
Slowly, ita melt all dem foundation away
Far mose, it mean starvaton, an wit no land fi sidung pan an call home,
som a drown
An all are bewilder and anxous
Ina dees stressful state, dem no go feel safe, so wont procreate.
Dis breakdown of nature
Mus be a tarture

It may sound like a tall tial mia tell
No sah, evidince infronta evrybady
Wia mash up wi worl

Ita one ting to disrepect and insult tru ignorance
But to gwaan in de face of science will prove fatal
Leaders of the world, mi yu all a unu
Afi respand to dis global crisis wi put on wi own lap
If nutn done, or not soon enough
Widout fanfear the god wia serve will appear

Mi done

JON MACKLEY

WALKING ON EGGSHELLS

The Departure

I saw the train depart
As I arrived at the station.
I cried "She is gone."
But the wind spoke to me,
      whispering, "She is on the train
            and the train is only gone from sight."

So I will write letters
      in the sand
            and hope that the sea
                  will wash them away
                        and carry them for you
                              to read them some day.

Going to the Moon

When things get tough
And I know they will
I think of John F. Kennedy
Who declared to the masses
In his best voice:
"I am also a doughnut".
He'll be remembered for that,
As well as being shot
In Dallas. Like J.R.

But he also said:
"We go to the moon.
Not because it is easy
But because it is hard."

Sometimes the greatest courage is found
In those who strive to overcome.
Those who say:
"Enough is enough".
Their plaintive voices
Shouted down by the crowds.
But *they* know they have said it
And have made their first stand.

Sometimes I want to say:
"I'm going outside; I may be some time."
But when we fight with our demons
Fight with age-old spectres
We are saying: we *can* get to the moon.
The lonely space between here and there
Needs a guide.

When engines fail and all hope seems lost
Say: "We *can* go to the moon.
Not because it is easy
But because
It is hard."

The Graveyard of the Damned

      Mist ground down in the valley.
Streetlights glisten like stars on the hillside,
Tiny reflections of their sisters in the night.
Birds conspire in low muttering.
The mountains are silhouettes in the distance;
      Blackened teeth of the giants.
Afternoon draws on and evening advances,
A gentle breeze kisses the back of his neck.
Wildlife swarms through the streets
At a peace with society which he no longer knows.

The sun now sleeps behind the mountains
Doused by the sea. Drowned by sorrows.
The skies explode in sprays
      Of gold, of orange and scarlet
      Bordered with the azure of salvation on one side,
And the shadows of damnation on the other.

There are few clouds in the skies tonight.
Behind him the mountains are prisons of rock
Clear as a vivid dream.
Scratches of white are ley lines in the sky.
      All converging on the point
      Where the sun has been laid to rest.

The lights of the valley are brighter now
      The lines which spiral down the mountain's side
      are orange snakes. They sparkle with malevolence.
Now the blankets of mist grow thicker.
Lights of glittering pearl join the serpent's deceit,
      And mingle with the lifeblood of the melting sky,
      Coruscating down the mountainside
The mountains which are the graves of the damned.

You might have seen me walking
(With acknowledgement to Bob Lind)

You might have seen me walking
Through the long-abandoned ruins
Of the man I used to be.
You might have seen me talking
To ghosts of ancient doings
Claiming my right to be me.
You might have watched in wonder
As I fought ghosts long laid to rest
Tearing ruined walls asunder
As they face the final test.

You might have seen me standing
At the crossroads of the present
Gazing at the reflection
Of the man I have become.
You might have seen me demanding
Of the man I now resent
On how I failed to pass inspection
When he demanded perfection
And did the best that could be done.
You might have asked the two men
Why they had argued just then
Instead of choosing the way
Or speculating on those not travelled
As twisted paths unravelled
As we step on the new path today.

You might have seen me stepping
Forward to the future, in trust,
Yet the future is no wide field
But an Abyss yawning before me,
And only faith allows another step.
You might have seen me forgetting

That faith might occasionally yield:
And still the Abyss retreats – it must,
For, although unseen, the path will always be.
You might have seen me speaking
To prophets of the future who tell
Of power and woe, of heaven and hell.
You might have heard me keeping
All those letters, never sent,
Or guilt for crimes already spent
And reflecting on ancient times gone by,
Of those ruined structures, destroyed by my
Shattered memories, torn and rent.
Or you might have seen me trying to piece
Together and salvage all that I can find
So that the poet may find his own release
And bring soothing to a troubled future mind

You might have seen me do all these,
For it is open for all to see
But before you judge, ask yourself, please
Are you sure that it was me?

Teardrops

I. I do not follow. I do not under
stand what this is all about.
I cannot grasp
the words you are saying.
And you. You keep on
talking. Giving me symbols that
I fail to interpret.
And you. You keep on saying
Saying your truth and I can't process.
And I. I am just trying. Trying
to hold on to my part of
reality.

And you. You keep on talking.
Talking in the strangest of illusions.
And I. I keep on thinking.
Thinking if I want the truth
I'd have asked for it.
And now. Now I see the darkness.
Looking beyond this world
but not seeing.
And I. I find this moment,
I'm crying in hell, but
no one's listening.
Because here,
my teardrops in hell
hold no
interest.

A place. A place where all
hope has left us. A place of
deception. A place where all
moments are frozen in crystal
already broken.

But tears. A teardrop in hell
is so meaningless
because everyone has one.
And I. If I'd wanted this abuse
I'd have listened
to the voices in my head.
And I. I need a moment.
To deliberate what
to do
now.

The Shooting Star
(For Jojo)

I saw a shooting star this morning
A quick burst of starlight
Steaking across the sky
A silver pin against night's velvet.
Blink and you miss it!
And I thought of you, my friend
How quickly it all passes
And we're left with twinkling memories.
Was it a moment where you called out
"Keep talking to me, because I am here"?
Or was it Heaven offering a teardrop for you
Because I have none left to give?

The Storm

The child looks out at the swirling clouds, dark and angry. "There's going to be a storm," he says. And the man nods. "It's going to be a big one," he says. "More than a day?" the child asks. The man nods. "More than a week?" And the man nods again. "More than a month?"

The man lays his hand on the child's shoulder. "It's a storm that'll last so long you can't see the end of it." "Will there be an end?" the child wonders. "Oh yes," says the man. "It will end. But on a day that you'll least expect it. When the waves have capsized then smashed your boat. When the storm is so furious that it tears your living breath from your body. When you've gone twenty thousand times past the moment that you think you can't take any more. THAT is when the storm will end."

He looks down sadly. "But the storm will be so long, that you'll forget that calm ever existed. It will be so violent you'll forget that anyone else sailed with you. Sometimes throwing yourself into the waves might seem like the better option than hoping the clouds will ever break."

"It doesn't sound like it'll be worth the effort," the child says. The man wipes away a tear, "It WILL be worth it," he says. "How do you know?" the child asks. The man looks away. "How do you KNOW?" the child asks again, angry now. "I have to BELIEVE," the man says. "Because I am the storm. And so are you."

The child looks at the clouds again. "I can't steer my boat through the storm alone." The man places his hands on the rudder. "No one said you had to be alone."

And the clouds roll.
And lightning flashes.
And thunder rumbles.
And the boat pitches.
And the child does not see the man any more.
Until he becomes him.

After the Storm

After the storm. After the night
Of rain lashing against rattling window panes,
Of trees violently hurling their branches,
And winds screaming through like lost children.
After the storm where no one dared go outside
But clung to each other for safety.
After the storm which ripped away buildings.
Tore away life. A storm that seemed
To go on forever. After THAT storm
When skies became the colours of an old wound
When the sun shines when it seems that
It would never shine again. After that storm
Where the survivors look around, bewildered
At the devastation left in its path,
After that storm which has levelled
Buildings, tearing up land and lives,
the people begin to rebuild,
Knowing that for the rest of the world
Nothing has changed. And for them
Nothing will be the same again.

The Visitor
(With acknowledgement to Derek Walcott)

I saw him today for the first time in years.
He is younger than I remember
And he welcomed me at his door
Of the house that is/isn't my own
And, as we embraced, tentatively at first,
I felt the warmth of a love I had forgotten.
And energy flowed into me
Filling me with a fire I had lost.
And there was no recrimination
Even when he asked "Why did you forget me?"

It wasn't conscious, of course,
But a gradual building of a wall
I never knew I was building
Block by block. And I blocked him from my life.
And he didn't blame me for the decisions I had made
Though he questioned some of my choices
But he shrugged and said "And that is how we learn."

And so we sat and we drank and we ate
Food, and I'd forgotten how it tasted,
Because it tasted of my youth.
All the time me looking at him looking at me.
He said: "I didn't think you would be so old now."

And I explained the things that had troubled me
Over years of unhappiness where I hadn't known
I was unhappy. He placed his hand on mine
And said "Live. Heal. And love yourself.
And come back to this moment."
After we had dined and supped he stood
And said "I am here for you."

And my heart filled with the grief
That only comes from kindness.
I realised the truth in those words –
The lantern in the darkness
The thread through the labyrinth
The crutch when I'm weakest.
The shoulder to cry on.
Sometimes time heals.
Sometimes kind words and deeds are the balm
To soothe the wounds of the person you've ignored
And a life you've forgotten.
Until then …
Until then.

The Cinema

I took you with me to the cinema
To watch a film that you weren't going to see.
We held hands, just as we didn't hold hands
On that first date that we never went on.
And afterwards, we talked, talked until dawn
Shared thoughts on everything we'd seen that day
And about all the things you didn't say
Just as you didn't once before. We spoke
Of things that were and those that might have been
And I thought of the words we would have said
About things you loved. Just like we didn't.
In the cinema, I still watched the film
You're sat with me, like my first date with you
Because that was a dream, and this is too.

Don't Ask …

Please don't ask how I'm feeling
Unless you can hear the answer.
You may see someone
Who is tired: quiet and withdrawn
Or someone who is moody and unsociable.
You ask me how I am, but, if I tell you
You'll hear what you want to hear.
        But:
        Inside my head are a
        Thousand voices shrieking
        Spiteful, jibing, accusing,
        Reminding me of
        Every guilty action I've done.
        Or I'm imprisoned, screaming,
        Crying, hurting, lost, lonely, lamenting,
        Mourning in tears that won't flow
        Frightened – so frightened – that
        The marrow inside my bones is trembling.
        I'm fighting a battle, a war, in silence
        And I'm clinging onto coping
        With breaking fingernails.
But that's seen as coping.

So if you ask how I am
Whatever I tell you, you'll hear
What you want to hear:

I'm fine.

My Library

The oldest book in my library.
It was a fragment of a childhood memory
A book I was never allowed to touch
(But secretly did, when no one was there.)
I loved the smell of the pages
And I loved the feel of the paper
And the sound the spine made as it stretched.
And I never read a single word.
And then, it vanished. After we moved house
I never saw it again.
But I was still a child. I didn't *miss* it,
Just wondered where it had gone
But didn't care enough to ask.
It was just tucked away in a corner of my mind,
A place I never needed to look.
And one day it appeared,
Hidden in a box stuffed full of memories
From a time before we moved.
I found it when I cleaned out my parents' attic
Put in a box, and never taken out again
And they weren't there to ask about it.
A book printed before
my grandfather's grandfather's was born.
The book smells good.
It smells of centuries and dust
And childhood memories of my parents' house.
But even now, I've never read a single word.

ROBIN OLIVER

HOME

Flying Lessons

I'd like to be a page pilot.
An instructor in a two-seater sensor.
Welcoming strangers in,
then demonstrating, my definition of flying.
Perhaps my temple is in the air,
on the wings of a carefully crafted sheet
of folded, rhymes, and verses.
To truly see the written word,
first requires height, altitude,
a willingness to bank above the clouds.
A journey does not need to be linear,
earthbound, or self-contained.
It's okay to spread someone else's wings,
and take to the sky.
This may not be where you were headed,
but so what if you can smile,
life is often best, when unexpected.
Trust me, and I won't just show you the view,
I'll pass the controls over to you,
and let you have a turn
at manoeuvring this shaky little plane.
Be brave, look straight down,
and you'll get my point of view,
Can you see how it fits together?
The pieces of a person,
littered throughout the landmarks?
It's like a giant jigsaw puzzle,
now you find the edges and the corners.

Sometimes the only way,
to stand back, is to take off,
find a point of reference,
and work inwards.
Trust what is invisible,
because if the elements and evidence,
are telling you you're moving upwards,
you might as well enjoy it.
Can you see where we started?
There's no denying that sort of distance.
The sound may never stop.
The clattering, rattling,
as the air scrabbles at the gaps,
in this rapidly aging aircraft,
but it's okay, it's still fit for purpose,
recently passed a full service.
The noise is just a realisation,
of everything we're pulling through.
It's time to explore.
We have all the room in the sky,
there are no wrong turns,
or ways to collide.
This flightpath is fully booked, and prepaid,
in all 360 degrees of airspace.
Please feel free to take these words for a spin,
see what each phrase, has been chosen to do,
and don't worry about the last line,
I'm an old pro.
I could land this beast with my eyes closed.
Only I won't, when I bring us down,
I'll kiss the ground,
like a man in prayer.
like someone who knows, the value of the earth
the dirt and the friction,
that finishes their descent.
As gravity pins us back, to the topography,
of everything we can, and cannot, leave behind.

New Home

Late September glares bright,
but the woods catch, soften the rays,
into something easier to see.
By my side, a rush of water.
An undercurrent,
to the flare and strobes,
of traffic noise.
So, I follow the flow,
further in, further away,
and there, four beautifuls display.
Wings that flick and flash,
shining, peacock blue,
jewels escaped,
from the restraints,
of a lifetime below.
And it's all new,
but it's old,
and I want it,
to be home

T Day

It's a surge of disbelief
a jolt of joy
the day, this day
is finally here
and my god
it's been such a long time coming.
An eternity, an entirety of past
of moments, all planted, seeded, in the wrong place.
Just weeds, in someone else's world
yet growing somehow surviving
in the shade, the chill, of overshadowed life,
but this here is hope
deeds to the house, keys to the door
a home, that truly can be your own.
Yours to do with as you will
paint the walls, with your dreams.
Fill the rooms, with bursts, sparks, and explosions
of man-made plans, ideas, and pulsing aspirations
for your future. A future you want
want to live within
to hold, run, jump, and dance
your way through all
its climates, storms, and hurricanes
because now you want
and you want to be
so, these are weeds no more, pests no longer.
These shoots, roots and buds have endured
stood, through freezing cold,
and wilted, yes, in the raging flames
of hell on earth
yet somehow green remained
and through luck, grit, or stubbornness,
resisted, held on, and didn't let go,

and this here
this is choice, this is freedom.
Fuel for the furnaces, that burn cool
within a heart, of a man
with his future reclaimed.
This here, is opportunity
this here, is real, honest
salvation.

Home coming

Someone else lived my past,
that's the thought I have,
as I stare at the photograph.
My memories are the only place,
where I share the same space,
as my brother's smiling face.
Lost property.
That's what it looks like,
feels like, somebody else's life.
Yet, I'm carrying the memories,
that make that statement a lie.
I wonder what I would have looked like,
Aged 20, but born a boy?
Aged 20, but out and proud?
Aged 20, and already transitioning?
I never met my grandparents,
as the real me,
I wonder what they would have said.
I can't seem to reconcile the pictures,
with how I perceive myself, in my head.
It's like, I was the only one
whoever really saw me,
and then only rarely.
It's like I had a sister,
a stand in, a stunt double, a place holder,
who was there when I couldn't be.
Who inhabited my form,
and inscribed my memories for me,
because that's the only thing I have,
that ties up, and doesn't lie,
that and the colour of my eyes.
These are the things,
that tell me, my past is true.

That I am the same person,
who lived that life, and grew
up, in that house.
With these people, and family,
from who I inherited,
so many traits and tendencies,
and here, is the evidence, framed,
like it is something to treasure.
To take care of, and look at with pride,
but all it does for me,
is cause my bile to rise.
My stomach to stir,
and nausea to interfere,
with the final task,
that has brought me here.
It's like the last line,
in a dot-to-dot picture.
Walking through the door,
under the title of mister,
and being back at the beginning,
but my grandmother's face is no longer here,
broadly grinning

Our Cry

Lines are violent, they divide us,
cleave the world to pieces.
Battle lines, front lines,
four corners and sides.
Clear cut labels,
boxes, that tell you who you are,
and who you aren't.
What you can and cannot be.
Who's team you're on, who's the enemy.
Who you should blame, ridicule,
and call name, after name, after name…

Yet, take a pen.
Draw faint, thick, sparse, spotted,
marks put to paper, and you tell me a story.
You show me a picture,
with shapes and hints, structure, and life.
So why not take a line, break it up, rub it out,
re-paint it clearer, brighter, bolder.
Use it, to make a form, climb upon it,
and shout your name.
Tell the world how it should be,
How these lines, are ours to mould,
to place, and to choose.
What do we want, how could it be?
Scratch out the lie,
that the past defines us.
Write on the clouded sky,
the truth, the hope, that in reality,
history holds only memory.
The future is ours.
Scribble it on the walls.
Graffiti the tarmac roads.

The roads that only ever told us,
the way we had to go,
and imagine saying "No!"
Use your mind's eye to see,
the bits, the pieces, weaved together.
Supporting each other,
aspiring to be better, fairer, kinder.
Take hold of your heart, and use it,
to rip, tear and fold, the world into a new shape.
Where you can find your home, your earth, your kin,
and dare to disagree, to fight, and scream
"You're doing it wrong, the way it is,
isn't the way, it always has to be!"

Emergence

Crawling out a hole.
Bare cold earth below,
but heat inside, within the core an engine.
Coming to life, fanning a flame,
a glow, a thirst, a need for movement, for action.
That fumbles forward, slipping, tripping,
yet standing again, temporarily slowed,
but still the vibration grows.
Humming, strumming,
spreading, flowing, to every part,
each limb feeding from a fiery heart.
Enticing, coaxing, wings to beat.
Faster, even faster still,
until the warmth breaks through,
the ground falls away.
Then free, free flying.

Hide

A cup of nothing
I held its fragile form in my hands.
It held its breath in its lungs.
A stillness as swift as death
no twitch or wrestle, just wait.
This tiny face
white, blue, and beak striped black
a buoy afloat the level of my grasp.
As I carry it out
together, open up.
Then it shoots like a rocket
disappearing into space.
The looping up kick of thrust
as its small wings throw it upwards.
A whirl of feathers and friction,
then gone.
Life no longer in my hands.
Us both
freer for the leaving.

City Escapes

I feel as if my limits, are a destination
that can be left, at any train station.
Distance, putting it between me and the past
and hoping the memories don't come back.
That's something to say,
a way to describe the anxiety.
Light glides, off the window
down the tracks
houses line the hills
like caterpillar backs
and the breath and rise
of estuary tides
cuts water into the land divide.
White clouds patchwork, the blue sky
and on the bank's, canopies surge by.
Everything has a temperature, at which it vibrates
a velocity that takes an engine to escape.
Striped by jet trails, fence rails
and rained streaked details
this is the cut-glass picture
onto which my breath exhales.
The grey morning grass
an ocean full of camera flash.
Haloed horses, in a jewellery box
the day a broach, upon my coat
pinned like treasure, to my chest.
In defence, diggers present arms
in the face, of salt spittled time.
Whilst a horn blast greets
the fading salute of children.
Can anyone defy wave action?
Mud flecked with avian lint
and within it all, three little egret.

Somewhere, along the line,
I think there was a lesson learnt?
Freedom of expression, within streets
unburden by oppression
and in other people's artifacts
I re-find the confidence I lack.
As these minutes are written,
and I turn around, on the record.
Light in the laughter
orange juice skyline
and the young ones are right
as we wait, held
shaking at the red stop light.
Puddles of life
framed by indoor edges
as blunt as the night.
A single star, a bright point
to wish upon a home
there's so much left unknown.
Air cut with a wheel squeak
money spent, into the hands
of a working week.
A man in the doorway
bowed head, can he really be asleep?
Then the Genting casino
and the erect, church spire behind it
Here, the obscenity, in the majesty
as I test my city limits
can I silence my inner critic?

Heart

Palm to my chest
I hold the power of this heart
within my grasp, beating.
It is in the mirror, quivering.
Not a portrait of a stranger
but my reflection.
Skin to skin
I feel the rhythm of reason.
A breath, no longer held
constricted and bound.
The distance between
me and myself
is here, in reach.
A silhouette
in genuine relief.

<h1 style="text-align:center">PAT PETTIT</h1>

<h2 style="text-align:center">DAMAGE LIMITATION</h2>

Jeremy glared at the screen of his Smartphone and re-read the text from his ex-girlfriend.

"Fetch all your belongings from my apartment this evening. I will not be there. When you lock up, post my keys, which you had promised to return, through the letter box."

The ultimatum which Jeremy had dreaded had arrived. He threw the mobile to the end of the settee on which he was sitting and leant back to study the patterns of discolouration on the ceiling of his bedsit. A lick of paint from the "one coat covers all" range would solve it, but nothing could rejuvenate jaded love. He punched the cushions into shape, rearranged them along the long settee, pattern, plain, red, grey, pattern, plain, red, grey. He emptied another black bin bag onto the floor, unfolding the woollen throw which she had given him last Christmas and throwing it over the spare chair in the corner of the room. He remembered being in their flat folding it so precisely into a smaller and smaller bundle to stuff into a black bin bag when she had asked him to leave.

Jeremy retrieved his phone, re-read the message and thought about how to reply. She had cheated on him, let him down, and dumped him by text and he did not want her to know that it mattered to him.

"Screw you," he said aloud.

"OK. 7.30," he texted.

That evening he arrived at the flat which they had shared for so many idyllic months. He remembered moving in two years ago on a cold January evening, throwing his clothes into the spare bedroom and being treated to a shared hot bath. Jeremy had known that his bachelor days were over. Loneliness swirled away with the soapy water as the bath emptied and warm towels enveloped him. That memory seemed like yesterday to him.

Jeremy knocked politely on the lounge door in the event she had stayed to see him for one more time. He entered the lounge. She wasn't there. A pile of his things was laid out in the middle of the room. He realised the finality of it and began moving the boxes out and down the stairs to his car with the speed of a burglar. He did not stop to look in any of them. He glanced around the room but did not want to be reminded of any details of their shared existence. He struggled with a larger box sliding it down the bottom three steps to the pavement then turned to enter the apartment for one last time. Jeremy had a further task to do.

He went into the kitchen and took off his watch. She would recognise it because she had given it to him. It was expensive and it had been very precious to him but their time together was gone. He wanted to destroy it like she had destroyed their life together. His anger coiled like a spring and the watch was no longer important to him. He wondered whether to put the watch in the washing up bowl and fill it up with water. He would wait for the second hand to stall but Jeremy realised that the watch was submersible to a certain depth. The second hand would continue its silent circle of minutes. If he put the watch on the kitchen floor and stamped on it he might be able to mark it with a slight scratch on the glass but the damage would be nothing compared to his hurt pride.

Jeremy smiled as he watched the second hand smoothly sweeping the circumference of the dial. He laughed aloud, a deep, short, harsh sound, echoing in the silent kitchen. The watch was moving on relentlessly as if nothing had changed. Moving on … He thought about it for a few moments. If he returned the watch to her, it would be like a symbol of the loving times they had shared. It would show her a certain constancy although he was reconciled to a period of time for them both moving on. Jeremy wiped the watch carefully on a tea towel, took it into the bedroom and carefully placed it on her pillow. He scribbled a few words on the notepad on the bedside table and placed it next to the watch – "Returned with love and as you look at it, I hope it reminds you that I think of you with every passing second."

He sat on the bed, head in hands for a few minutes then left the apartment, pushing the keys through the letter box, as arranged.

Meantime, the watch stopped.

A deep lane connected the farmhouse with the main road which led to the village. Maidenhead ferns and ancient twisted trees dripped their moistness onto the hedgerow below sending trickles of muddied water flowing into the rutted gutters on either side of the lane.

The fields above this ancient cutting had seen generations of farmers ploughing, tilling, scything and harvesting in an annual treadmill and every week since the Lord of the Manor had released his serfs to freedom, a pilgrimage to market had processed along this deep lane.

Jane drove her old Morris van carefully uphill, staying to the centre of the lane to avoid the potholes. It was a tortuous mile and a half from the farmhouse to the main road and a further mile to the village shop where she was taking several boxes of eggs for sale. She dropped down into first gear on the sharp bend as the tyres slid into the runoff from the fields and gently pulled away to preserve the cargo of eggs balanced in the back of the van.

She reached the main road at last and within five minutes was able to park outside the old post office and village shop.

"Morning Mrs Foster. Got anything for me today?"

"Hello Jane – yes as a matter of fact, I have. A parcel from Australia addressed to the occupier of Valley Farm. That's you – now that you're on your own like. Here you are. Only small but as a matter of fact, precious things comes in small packages, that's what my old dad used to say."

"Thank you, Mrs Foster. Strange. I don't know anyone in Australia. Well I'll just bring in the rest of the eggs for you and I'll be off. Work to do."

It was several hours later, after a quick supper and check of the animals before Jane opened the parcel. Beneath the paper was a worn cardboard box. Jane stared at it. She recognised it instantly and was overwhelmed by an intertwining of negative emotions. Taped on top of the box lid was a short note. She searched around for her reading glasses, scattering a pile of paperwork from the kitchen table on which she was leaning. She sat down to read the note overcome by a sudden weakness in her legs. Jane read it out loud.

"These artefacts may belong to your family. Let me know if you recognise the objects, the names or the people in the photograph. Regards, Phillip Mason." Jane noted that the address was in Perth, Western Australia. There was a phone number and an email address. She read it again, searching for some bonding or inter-connection with the writer whose name she did not recognise. Who was he? How had he found out her contact details?

Intrigued, she opened the box, unwrapping a small quantity of bubble wrap and then some crumpled yellowed tissue paper which was protecting the objects. Because she already guessed what she would find, Jane took her time to carefully unwrap the items. At the moment she found herself holding a baby's crocheted bootee in pink wool she began to sob. Inside the bootee, for added protection, was a small pottery candle holder inscribed with the words "To light you to bed." For several moments she quietly let the tears flow unchecked. Lying flat on the bottom of the box were several black and white photographs which Jane examined, wiping away the tears to look at each one in turn.

She tried to untangle her thoughts. She recognised each item, and each of the faded images. Forty-five years was a long time to harbour such feelings as had been evoked by the sight of the contents in the box from Australia – guilt, sadness, anger, helplessness. For a moment she was swept away like the mud from the banks of the deep lane, her peace of mind eroding with a landslide of poignant memories. Her love affair, his betrayal, his leaving, the heartache, the disgrace, the baby, the adoption and the severing of all links with her beloved daughter and yet more heartache and interminable loneliness.

Jane composed herself and sat down at her laptop. What connection was Phillip Mason to her daughter, she wondered? Husband? Stepbrother? Son, even? "Maybe I have a grandson" Jane mused. There must be a family connection for him to have seen these objects and to know the address of the farm. Jane felt that she could not afford to connect with the suppressed emotions of yesteryear. She felt strangely curious yet uninvolved. It had been too long ago. She typed a quick email response to Phillip apologising for her lack of information about the people in the photographs, and offering to return the contents of his parcel to him.

Before she re-wrapped the parcel for its return to the village post office, she took the objects up to her bedroom. Opening the second drawer of her dressing table, she took out a matching pink bootee and paired them together. So long apart. Next she found the other pottery candle holder and placed each alongside the other so that they read "Here is a candle" and "To light you to bed".

Jane appreciated the togetherness of the items and how incomplete they had always seemed without their connecting partner. A pair of bootees and a pair of pottery candle holders should always have been together, yet circumstances had not allowed that. She considered the intervening years of separation and the thousands of miles which had kept them apart and decided to send all four objects back to Phillip in Australia. They stayed in that position for the very first time in nearly fifty years. The next morning Jane re-packed the parcel with the four items and having clearly addressed it, placed it carefully on the back seat of her van to take it back to the village Post Office. The potholes in the deep lane leading away from her farm demanded her entire concentration yet Jane drove confidently towards the village knowing that at last a sense of closure awaited her.

SAM RICHARDS

THE BOOK OF SAM (UEL)

The New Normal

In the new normal
Everyone will see the dawn,
Hear the birds sing,
Understand the words of their songs,
Stroll through mornings and afternoons
Like a slow piano drag
And at the end of the day,
See the sunset
And fall in love again:
The new normal
Is a place of wonder.

In the new normal
The lion and the lamb
Will step the light fandango
Swigging a brighter shade of ale,
Presidents, premieres and prime ministers
Will learn the steps
Stiffly at first
But when they find their feet
Will smile new smiles
That they last smiled
When they were little babies:
The new normal
Is a place of love
And wonder.

In the new normal
Everyone will be cared for –
The more care you need
The more you get.
The slogan will be:
Care is not just for Christmas –
It's in the air we breathe,
All we eat, all we drink in
And everyone will get peaceburgers
With extra fries –
No exceptions,
All free, gratis
And served with great big ladles of good will
And loving spoonfuls of rock and roll,
Jazz and boogie.
The new normal
Is a place of innocence,
Love and wonder.

In the new normal
We'll all care about what we can't see
As much as what we can,
And we'll know that what we can see
Is made by what we can't;
The air will be clear,
The sea will be fresh and strong,
Pollution will be taught about
In history books,
Safe, clean energy
Will give us clean, safe energy
For living our lives.
The new normal
Is a place of life,
Innocence, love
And wonder.

In the new normal
Politicians will be fitted with lie detectors,
There will be public health warnings
On all election addresses,
Banks will be turned into pleasuredomes,
The Foreign Office will be staffed by foreigners
There'll be jobs to spare
Because everyone's happy without them,
Teachers will be taught by children,
Capitalism will be the dirty underwear
You left under the bed ages ago
And is now gathering fluff,
Religions will be left to get on with it
As long as they let the rest of us get on with it too,
Universities will pay students to attend,
Work will be abolished
And no one will miss it,
Conspiracy theorists will get their brains back – unwashed,
Where there was money there'll be music
You'll never get to the end of the lollipop
And the new normal
Is a place of delight,
Life, innocence, love
And plenty
And plenty
And plenty of
Wonder.

Licence to Thrill

I flashed my poetic licence
And the sumo wrestler called Les
Who never smiled
Let me in
Through the improbable door
Into the poem's hinterland
Smack whack bang in the lounge
Of the country mansion
That belonged to the zillionaire
Without a face
And a big sneer.

The bass walked,
The drums brushed
A cracked sax was lost in the mist,
And the radio had been left on.

She sat there on a high stool
By the drinks cabinet
With her film noir legs
Showing me a good time –
Told me I'd need a good stiff
Drink.

In the corner was a statue of Venus;
I struck a match on its arse,
Lit a Kent
And cased the joint
For hidden cameras –
There was one above the bed -

There was a white grand piano
With a guy called Sam
Who kept playing it again
And again;
The clock showed half past nothing –

No time to lose
But it refused to chime
Without a bribe.

No one could be trusted in that haunted house;
The butler was a hit man
The cat sat on the mat
Spat
And exploded
Just missing me by a cigarette paper.

Then they burst in –
All ten of them -
Machine guns blazing
But I shot 'em all
With one bullet,
Wiped off my revolver
Tucked in my shirt,
And looked back to the high stool.
She was gone …

I took out my phone
And spoke to S:
Mission accomplished, I whispered under my breath.
Came the answer:
Get out now –
There's a helicopter on the lawn,
Get in it – now!
As we flew away
The whole place went up in flames.

If you don't believe me
Come over here,
Make sure no one sees
My licence –
It's secret and
Very poetic –
Cross my heart and hope to fly
High …

If You Could Buy a Revolution

If you could buy a revolution
We'd have had one by now.
If you could market the world turned upside down
It would happen every week
Buy two get one free.
The box set would be cheap at the price,
The theme tune would be sung by Rhianna
With her East-is-Red Umbrella ella,
It would be serialized on Channel Four,
The Daily Mail would be on the floor
Up shit creek
Without an oar,
It would make you happy,
Cool and snappy,
It would go well with early evening cocktails
And discourses about post-post modernism
On the wind-swept piazza of life.
It would get us out of the wood
Abolish the word should
We'd be dancing round the neighbourhood
Finger lickin' good.

If you could buy a revolution
Everyone would want one,
They'd work harder to get theirs.
No one would want to be the sad reactionary kid
Who got left out
And has no friends on Instagram.
It would be the next in style,
Make you smile,
Joyful as a computer file,
It would be the must-have for the streetwise gotall
Who must have everything;
Girls with ride or die lips
Semi-permanent insurgent eye shadow
And guerrilla razor cut hair
Would make a stand on street corners

With incendiary manifestos
And distribute them in the heat of the moment,
Hitch up their skirts
And sit down in front of the traffic
On their way to Monroes to arrest the bouncer.

If you could buy a revolution
Advertising agencies would flog it worldwide
Rebrand it from dour sourpuss old Marxism
Make it sweet
Move your feet
To the heat of the beat
Of the Means of Production rap – yo;
It would be targeted at
The Amaze generation
And generate amazement
In the under fifteens
From each according to their means.

If you could buy a revolution
It would replace Disneyland
As the happiest place on earth,
You could *just do it* in your insurrectionary Nike trainers,
Purchase it with a surprising uprising Master Card,
Go pick it up in the ultimate driving machine
Keen and mean,
Take it home
Out of the box
And watch it snap crackle and pop
In 50 shades of gay.

If you could buy a revolution
The winner would sing
The People's Flag
Signed up by Comrade Simon Cowell,
Richard Branson would move the Politbureau
To the British Virgin Islands,
And People's Friend Alan Sugar would tell capitalism:
You're fired!

It would be enfranchised
Privatized, advertised,
Incorporated, regulated
Syndicated in 32 countries
In more languages
Than you can shake a profit margin at;
It would be outsourced, endorsed
Actively managed
By development directors on the make
With an eye for a tax break
Like so many snakes
In the grass
Where recuperation comes to pass
Who would make sure
The first are still first and the last stay last,
While we watch the kids
Finally free from school
Cool as a credit crunch
Doing what comes naturally.

If you could buy a revolution
We'd all be happy
As a glass of champagne
A supermarket chain
Or a capital gain.
It would come
With a three day money-back special offer.
It would enter into an insubordinate merger
Organized by rioting bankers
And loony left gangsters
From international finance houses
And tax havens populated by patriots
Who'd seen which side their bread's buttered
And stopped droning on about loyalty
And royalty
And all things trite and dutiful
And talk about something interesting instead.
You could see it on replay

A smash on Broadway
Every day a May Day
Is everybody happy?
You bet yer life we are.

If you could buy a revolution
It would give you sex appeal
For free
And be sploshed all over your body
As you swagger out
Into the fashionable rebel downtown
Get pissed anarchist
Nighttime midnight
People's republic of
Every little helps
Where everyone's got the T shirt
And supermarketed ripped jeans.

If you could buy a revolution
There wouldn't be a lonelyheart in sight:
No Queen of the Night
Would be seeking
Her very own Mozart
For a little night musik;
Big Ben would tell the Bank of England
I've got the time if you've got the money;
It would be witty in company,
A Good Sense Of Humour -
It would be entertaining
Never complaining
Never fart
Or pick its nose
In company;
Cheerful as a current account
And jolly ho ho as a trade discount.

If you could buy a revolution
It wouldn't be a revolution
Now would it…

A Peace Grenade

I'll tell you what I want
I want a peace grenade
A peace grenade
I'd pull out the pin with my teeth
And roll it quietly into war zones
And it would explode everywhere
In every corner
In every tank
In every armoured car
And leave a trail of reconciliation
And happy confused people
In its wake

I want a peace grenade
I'd chuck it around so it landed
In every tyrant's Corn Flakes
And it would fizz joy and sunshine all over them.
I'd strap three to my middle
And set them off one by one
In a crowded street
With people from different religions either side of the road
And they'd be dragged into the light
Bleeding contentment
And screaming love of each other
All over the pavement.

I'll tell you what I want
I want a peace grenade
I want a whole box of them
Paid for out of taxes
To scatter them indiscriminately
Everywhere;
I'd rain them from the skies over Syria,
Blast them from a love rocket into the eye of ground zero
And spray them from a great height
Throughout the burning fields of poverty
The Pentagon
And battlefields everywhere.

I want a peace grenade
I want a whole consignment
I want to fling them around at random
In mindless acts of harmony.
I'd shove one up Vladimir Putin's arsehole
And watch him smile
For the first time in his life.
I'd release their contents as harmless gasses
Spray the crops with them
Spray the cops with them
I'd chuck one in their faces
And watch it explode all over them with a smile
I'd stockpile them and create a permanent peace economy
Based on no money, no profit, no investment
I'd give them out to kids to fling at bullies
And their teachers when they gave them exams and tests.
I'd plant them in shops
Timed to go off at the busiest time of day
And not give any warning.
And I'd watch them blow stars in the eyes
Of guilty bystanders
Who would suddenly learn to dance
And sing.
I'd put them on trains,
In the underground,
On rooftops
And up blind alleys.
Politicians would be obliged to swallow them whole.
The army would be sent home
Because the enemy would be lying around smoking them
And getting high as kites.
I'll tell you what I want
I want a peace grenade
A peace grenade
A peace grenade
A calm bomb
A goodwill rocket
A land-to-air love missile
A love-a-ton bomb
A peace grenade

Existentialism

I'm not here to do the washing up –
elbows in the sink
doin' the dirty water Fairy Liquid stomp –
that's not what I'm here for.
You know those old tales
about a lost soul
condemned to empty a bottomless pool
with a walnut shell with a hole in it –
that's the washing up,
right?
That's exactly it
and I'm not here to do it.

I can see those faces
on those big round nasty plates
poking their tongues out at me
chuckling like an in-the-sink gathering
of little devils
on loan from a Hammer Horror.
Well they can wash themselves –
shitpots.

I'm not here to do the washing up
or wipe down and polish surfaces
so you can see your face in them
and feel godly about it,
or do the laundry
or hoover the house from top to bottom
or sweep down the stairs.
I'm not here to fill in forms
or make trips to the recycling
in a car that's not big enough to hold it all,
or put the bloody bins out every week,
or go round fate-worse-than-death Morrisons
with a trolley with a wonky wheel,
or take the seagull shit motor

through the car wash,
or take the evidence of last week's drinking
to the bottle bank.
This is not what I'm here for.

I'm here to snooze as I choose
in a gentle hammock
in the cloudless summer sun
with a massive G&T with loads of ice,
to read whatever I fancy
for as long as I fancy
and not finish it if it starts to bore me.
I'll go inside across the lawn
if I feel like it
sit at my Bosendorfer
and play some Satie or Jelly Roll Morton,
eat huge grapes, *fruit de mare* for dinner,
out of this world vino
(none of your supermarket plonk)
maybe write some music
or a poem,
have an afternoon nap
then get up,
dress snazzy,
go to the opera with my wife
and after that
the two of us dine out in outrageous places
where only the outrageous go,
taxi home,
silk sheets on the bed,
dream till midday.

That's what I'm here to do.
That's
what
I'm here
to
do.
Anything else is a compromise.

Things That Have Been Said About My Piano Playing

your music is dead cool
your music is half full not half empty
your music just pours out of you
your music is like a trance
your music goes on a bit
your music tells me a lot about you
your music sucks
your music reminds me of Japan
your music makes me wet
your music takes a while to get going doesn't it
your music makes me really miserable
can't you play something we all know?
your music ain't got no tune
your music takes the biscuit
your music wouldn't go down in church
your music is on drugs – must be…
your music won't make you rich
your music sounds like my mother's got her tits in the mangle
go on play Take Five
your music would sound good a mile away
your music makes our cat seem like Pavarotti
your music really needs listening to or you just miss it
your music is like a broken clock – it can't keep time
your music makes me see things
your music is drunk in charge of a piano
your music reminds me of birdsong
or maybe an elephant honking
your music isn't exactly Mozart
d'you know any Kylie numbers?
your music is the soundtrack to a trip on a magic carpet
your music sticks it one to the wankers
your music gives as good as it gets
I'm not sure whether your music is Heaven or Hell
(it has elements of both)

your music is a form of abuse
your music lightens my load
as I trudge onwards on this daily journey through life
your music wouldn't win any prizes
I think you just make it up as you go along -
do you get paid for doing this?
your music shouldn't be allowed
you can't dance to it can you
unless you're an octopus;
your music isn't quite like anything else
your music really tickles my keys baby
I prefer Elvis
your music should be on telly
your music doesn't give a tinker's cuss or a flying fuck
your music goes forwards and then backwards doesn't it
(sort of like this)
why aren't you better known or known at all?
your music takes me back to my childhood
I once knew someone who played like that
oh you haven't finished have you?
encore!
your music says no to the big boys in the music industry
yes OK
– I'll take that last one

This is a poem

This is a poem.
It is not the will of the people -
The people have not spoken
For it – or for anything else -
Nobody voted for it –
Neither roughly one half nor roughly the other,
I just wrote it on no authority whatsoever;
It gladly has no authority
And nothing to deliver to anyone
And is bored at the prospect,
It doesn't bully anyone
Or shout louder than other poems.
It does not spit and sputter tired old clichés
About democracy
Or some such camouflage
For the state we're in.
It is a poem:
No one asked it to be written;
And no one knows
Whether it's desirable or not -
And who cares?
(Not me …)
There isn't a date
When it has to be read by
After which it can't be extended
Without upsetting a lot of people
Who deserve to be upset.
It could go on for ever
If it wants –
(Or not)
And there's nothing you can do about it.
No one will resign because they don't like it
Or look silly losing their temper on TV
Or call other poems names –
Such as: down with hosts of foreign waving daffodils!
With sell-out sonnets that cost taxpayers' money

That we could spend on armaments instead,
The transitional rhyme of the Euro-Mariner
And the Article 50 albatross death cult,
Or Do Not Go Gentle
Into That Good Backstop.

This is a poem:
If you don't like it
Leave it alone
But don't go on about it for God's sake.
It is not in the national interest
And there's no point pretending it is;
It is not interested
In the national interest
And the national interest
Has no interest in poems anyway.
A million people will not march in its favour.
A million people will never know of it
Thank goodness.

This is a poem:
It is what it is;
It is not buried under an avalanche
Of half-truths, no truths and weasel words;
It has never been plastered
On the side of a bus;
No money has been overspent on it.
It has no borders:
Anyone can read it - or not read it,
No one will lose their job by reciting it out loud.
It will not stop supplies getting through
Or piss off the Irish
Or suck up to American presidents.
No one feels it should be the subject
Of a peoples' vote
Mainly because it doesn't know who or what
The people are
And doesn't trust those who say they do.

This is a poem
It is not a saucer
It is not a clock
Nor is it a flying saucer
Never mind a flying clock
It is not a Member of Parliament
Or the episode of Coronation Street
That I missed last week
It does not walk backwards on all fours
Nor does it sink when waterlogged
It is a poem
Pure and simple
Without weight
Measurable dimensions
Or theoretical justification
It does not wear mascara
And it will never pay taxes
Although the person who wrote it does
It has never been to school
And doesn't regret it
The person who wrote it however
Has been to school
And has mixed feelings about it
This is a poem
It doesn't have wings or legs
Therefore it can't fly or run
Or kick anyone
Other than metaphorically
It doesn't believe in God
Nor does it not believe in God
God isn't an issue for it
Nothing is
Whether or not it is published
Has no bearing on the fact
That it is a poem
Nor on whether it's any good or not

It is a poem
Not a snake
Not a flat tyre
Not a box of chocolates
Not an old spanner
Not a sailor's hornpipe
Not a particular view of history
Not a failed love affair
Or a tentpole
It is not Kenny Knight
It is a poem
A poem
A poem
That's all
A poem

The Old is Dying and the New Can't Be Born
(Antonio Gramsci)

Now is the time of monsters -
Mutant monsters
Caught in their own traps
Of undead shadows from the days
When they were figureheads
On the bows of proud ships
Fixed on new horizons to plunder,
Ploughing the waves,
Teaching the natives not to be restless,
Teaching them cricket
Rule Britannia, Britannia sucks your blood
Now singing with the ghosts and ghouls
Of the last night of the Proms

Heigh ho, the moon in the morn
The old is dying and the new can't be born

Stand up, stand up for memories of glories
That you never lived through anyway –
That were dead before you were conceived
But you cling to by your fingernails
And call it Us, Ours
And now it's called History -
Not hers and certainly not theirs,
And had you been there
You'd have known all about the noise,
The early deaths, the diseases,
The uprooting and looting –
But rather you tell
Fairy tales of civilization
Slaying dragons
Not mentioning
Spreading God, fraud, wages
And the pox.

Those were the days
When little boys swept your chimneys
And whores were grateful
And black people wore striped trousers
And played banjos in the street -
Rule Britannia, Britannia turns it back
Makes its pile for this sceptred isle –
One God
One colour
One big happy family –
Right?

So it's heigh ho, here's your little bit of corn
The old is dying and the new can't be born

But don't you know
There's a kick inside the womb -
Can you feel it?
And it dreams of coming out and seeing
A clear, sheer big blue sky -
No orders, no borders,
Leaving the blood and guts of the earth in the ground
Where it belongs
And stop nicking them with your bloody great drills
And thinking you don't have to pay –
With the first cry of birth
From real breathing lungs
There'll be no more Earth's revenge –
Flood, fire, storm, disease,
Mutants, pollutants, cockup, lockup –
Rule Britannia, Britannia's in the way
So if you don't know how to help
At least don't act stupid –
'Cause the monkeys now refuse
To do their tricks
Or climb their sticks
Any more…

So it's heigh ho, are you rose or are you thorn?
Get the old out of the way so the new can be born

Heigh ho, Parliament Square
Sing a song of business,
Energy and industry –
Silly old buggers don't even know they're obsolete,
Unaware that for the angels glued to their buildings,
Blocking up the roads
It's deadly personal.
Unaware that depression and ennui
Are acts of rebellion
That can't be medicated by a nice job,
More wages or universal credit;
The old doesn't know that the new does know that
Being told to wait is a political plot
And has rumbled it;

So heigh ho, the shearers and the shorn
Are ready for the light, ready to be born

ROGER SCHIFF

POEMS FOR A TERRIBLE, BEAUTIFUL
AND MYSTERIOUS WORLD

The Lonely Poet

Written for the Poetry Evening for the Shekinah Mission MAY 2019
References to Clive and his dog Geezer who sells the Big Issue outside
Plymouth Theatre
Paul sells The Big Issue outside the Vodaphone Shop
Diana and Olwen joint founders of Shekinah Mission
John Bird founder of the Big Issue Organisation
A Syrian Refugee who I met, training to be a doctor after his father
tried to force him to kill Christians.

WHO ARE YOU?
I am a lonely poet sir wandering the Earth
Searching for truth looking to the skies
Mining for words in a word full of lies.

Unable to sleep I begin to pray, thinking of the people I met today.
Homeless man, cold and dejected, silently shouting 'I've been rejected'.
Empty buildings indifferently stare, lonely people a world that doesn't care.
Is Plymouth a town without pity? Where's the night shelter in this city?
The Good Samaritan had nothing to hide, not to pass by on the other side.

WHO ARE YOU?
I am a lonely poet sir, Wandering the Earth.
Searching for truth looking to the skies.
Mining for words in a world full of lies.

221

Unable to sleep I begin to pray, thinking of the people I met today.
Feeding our minds watching TV, sound judgement is not to be seen.
"Homelessness a big issue," said John Bird. 'My idea needs to be heard,'
Paul, standing alone, sells the Big Issue outside the shop, Vodaphone,
Outside so cold like being in a freezer, Clive with dog named Geezer.

WHO ARE YOU?
I am a lonely poet sir, wondering the Earth,
Searching for truth, looking to the skies.
Mining for words in a world full of lies

Unable to sleep I begin to pray, thinking of the people I met today.
I stopped to buy a tasty falafel and met a refugee talking family battles.
'Kill those infidels', his Father said, Paradise is yours, when you are dead',
'Such counsel will cause endless strife, wisdom from God must bring life.
'Thank you, Plymouth now I can see, air of freedom blowing from the sea'.

WHO ARE YOU?
I am a lonely poet sir wondering the Earth,
Searching for truth looking to the skies,
Mining for words in a world full of lies.

Unable to sleep, I began to pray,
Thinking of the people I met today.
Two women praying one cold night,
Homeless provision, can't be right.
Shekinah Mission born the next day.
Years later, mission going strong,
Diana and Olwen, not get it wrong.
Politicians notice. Do you really care?
Shekinah Mission flourishing, still there.

WHO ARE YOU?
I am a lonely poet sir wondering the Earth,
Searching for truth looking to the skies,
Mining for words in a world full of lies.

Gathered
Written May 2019 to commemorate the Rwanda Genocide

A sunny afternoon, brooding anguished sky,
Heavens darkened, the simple question why?
Gathered to remember, thousands who died,
So many Lord, Rwanda, judgement was nigh.

What could he add? the Lord Mayor had to say,
After all the horror we had heard about that day.
Auspicious occasion, sun fled, the sky was grey,
What to do? The Mayor's tears showed the way.

Words were spoken to introduce the occasion,
Remember the tragedy that befell that nation.
African blood crying out for justice to the Lord,
Bible says do not kill, where was God's sword?

We are good at fighting, said a Labour Party MP,
Good at war and fighting, peace much difficulty.
A Bishop spoke of forgiveness, warnings to heed,
They came for the Jews, then they came for me.

All the way from Rwanda, a woman who survived,
We heard of murdered families, being buried alive.
Rwandan High Commission, machetes and knives,
Foreign interference, indifference, ruined lives.

What could he add? The Lord Mayor had to say,
After all the horror we had heard about that day.
Auspicious occasion, sun fled, the sky was grey,
What to do? The Mayor's tears showed the way.

A Walk Through the Wood
An attempt to ponder the mystery of time

Standing under the old oak tree,
A magical place I happened to be.
That wizard called Time, I sought,
Things beyond means of thought.
Life is short my Mother used to say,
Yet the love of God is new each day.

Under that shady tree I stood,
Passing time in that ancient wood.
One glance at the book called Fate!
What's ahead on some future date?
Anxious for tomorrow, deceptive time,
Fully alive today, tomorrow will be fine.

Under that shady tree I stood,
Time Bells Japan, that ancient wood.
Inescapable, determined, vast reality,
Time fierce guardian of life's mystery.
Waking up in Tokyo life begins again,
Eastern wisdom, not Honda but Zen.

Under that shady tree I stood,
Neath starry skies in that ancient wood.
Space and time are curved Einstein said,
Quantum mechanics, impossible in head.
Everlasting God beyond space, endless time,
This thing called theology blows your mind.

Under that shady tree I stood,
Life nasty and short in that ancient wood.
A day to be born, work, then a time to die,
Time to relax, eat steak and kidney pie.
I may be ill, weak, find it difficult to speak,
Love God and neighbour this coming week.

Under that shady tree I stood,
Wondering about creation in that ancient wood.
Thirteen billion years, since big bang, they say,
Methinks, Genesis says this in a Biblical way.
'Formless, void, darkness' says the ancient text,
Creation ex nihlo, God's creative voice came next.

Under a shady tree I stood,
Seeking understanding in that ancient wood.
Adequate perception of religion Augustine said,
Faith before understanding, heart before head.
In the beginning was the Word then it all began,
What was time before God spoke, created man?

Under a shady tree I stood,
Pondering existence of evil in that ancient wood.
Jesus, no other good enough, pay the price of sin,
He only could unlock the gate of Heaven, let us in.
Procrastination steals our years until all are fled.
Time to pray, call on God, spiritual life, Jesus said.

Under that ancient tree I stood,
Time flies by fast in that ancient wood.
A killer rehearses, his murderous stabbing skills,
He's been deceived now in prison, time to kill.
I've been deceived, like Brexit I've been had,
Let's stop complaining, wake up and be glad.

Standing under the old oak tree,
A magical place I happened to be.
That wizard called Time, I sought,
Things beyond means of thought.
Life is short my Mother used to say,
Yet the love of God is new each day.

Numbers

What's the time nearly nine,
Hang your knickers on the line.
If a policeman comes along,
Take them off and put them on.

1 potato, 2 potato, 3 potato 4,
You'll get too fat if you ask for more.

There are only 3 steps to Heaven,
Eddie Cochran once said.
Be careful, only 1 heartbeat from Hell,
Then you are dead.

1, 2, 3, 4, 5, once I caught a fish alive,
6, 7, 8, 9, 10, then I put it back again.
1, 2, 3, got fed up had a nice cup of tea.

1, 2, buckle my shoe,
3, 4, knock on the door.
5, 6, 7, 8, 9, one knock would be just fine.

Get your kicks on Route 66,
Traffic jams, M25.
Gonna be late A38,
Don't take the train,
Dawlish again.

27 Counties in the EU,
Boris Johnson said 26,
That will certainly do.
Article 50 Parliament voted one day,
2019 a bad year for Teresa May.

400 years since the Pilgrim Fathers,
400 years later take the cobbles away.
400 years Plymouth has been neglected,
Walking up Union St it seems that way.

£350 million out of Europe into NHS,
It's a no brainer people said.
As the neurosurgeon moved from Britain,
I'll live in Paris he said.

10 Downing Street a nice address,
Living there gives you much stress.
Boris Johnson take a good long rest,
Soon you'll need a bullet proof vest.

No man can serve 2 masters
Jesus taught one fine day,
Doesn't apply to me, Dr Jekyll would say.
As the evil Mr Hyde gave him away.

6 million Jews dead.
1 million Cambodians dead.
1 million Rwandans dead.
1 million African slaves dead.
6 million aborted babies dead.
Million, can't get that number out of my head.

72 years since I was born.
72 years since that September morn.
72 years born in 1946.
72 years old.
Must learn some new tricks.

111 Grosvenor Road.
46 Parfett Street.
36 Ashington House.
129 Sandford Close.
406 Central Park Road.
North Hill Maldon.
6 Dandelion Close.
1 Flora Gardens.
12 Cremyll View.
So many things I've been through.

Elliot Terrace

A poem written to record the Unity Festival held in June 2019 on the Plymouth Hoe.

No way Osea said the town official,
'Can you use Plymouth Hoe in such a trivial way'?
The Lord spoke, as prayers were said,
'Its OK Osea,' you can now go ahead.

Elliot Terrace is famous to be sure.
Conan Doyle lived there many years before,
Sherlock Holmes, the Hoe by the seashore.
Lady Astor, the famous local woman MP,
Lived there too, looking out to the sea.
Bowling green not far away. It is often said,
Francis Drake played there, battle ahead.
War memorials covered with local names,
Worthy of remembering. Worthy of fame.
Plymouth Hoe, a special place for us to be,
A great Christian festival down by the sea.

Elliot Terrace, is famous to be sure,
Black and white together equal and free,
It's a pity John Hawkins is not there to see.
From Rwanda, Ethiopia, Kenya, Eritrea too,
These African people knew just what to do.
From across Britain, many people fat and thin,
The Hoe came alive as people started to sing.
'Go Plymouth Osea, said the vision in the night,
'Flee from fire of Rwanda, things will turn out right'.
Plymouth Hoe, special place for God's people to be,
In front of Elliot Terrace, a special place by the sea.

Elliot Terrace, is famous to be sure,
All that preaching and praying all around,
Band played loud; we were on Holy Ground.
African people, made Plymouth their home,
They saw the homeless, then heard their groans.
From so far away yet caring for Plymouth's needy,
Teaching us a lesson, teaching us not to be greedy.
It's OK Osea, come and teach us to live, be united,
A great man and from Africa, God's true anointed.
Plymouth Hoe, that June Day the 10th anniversary.
In front of Elliot Terrace, a special place for us to be.

No way Osea said the town official,
'Can you use Plymouth Hoe in such a trivial way'?
The Lord spoke, as prayers were said,
'Its OK Osea', you can now go ahead.

RETURN TO EXMOUTH

It was a glorious day in the Summer of 2020 when we caught our train to the beautiful resort of Exmouth. We went by train from Plymouth Station. As we sped through the August countryside the beauty of Devon kept passing by. Infinite sweetness as fertile valleys rushed past my weary eyes. Thirsty I drank deeply from the cup of beauty from this magical land of fields, trees, cattle, and sheep.

Exmouth was alive with visitors after the long shutdown. People's faces smiled with the surprise of good weather and open shops and cafes. All was well with the world as we sat, ate and drunk tea and coffee.

I felt at peace as I walked through the subway leading from the station. There was a man begging, clearly his mind in a different world to ours. A recovering drug addict he reminded me that it is good to enjoy life, but we must not use it to escape from reality. I read the words on the war memorial which talked of uneasy peace and savage yesteryear. I saw a burnt-out café with a police message talking about arson. Then I remembered the news on TV about youths fighting on the beaches of Exmouth. It was 75 years since we dropped an atomic bomb on Japan.

Could I sustain my peace in this quiet beautiful town with gentle shops and a beach full of people refreshing themselves in the sea? The words on the memorial UNEASY PEACE signalled to me my feelings on this bright summer's day. I sat down and wrote a poem using the word remembering the suffering and sacrifices of soldiers and others during the First and Second World War. The troubles of the world are always there, and we have lived for many years under the threat of nuclear war, menace of drug addiction and the restless nature of youngsters who want to fight. The challenge to love one another is always relevant. I sat down and wrote a poem to remind us of the suffering and sacrifice of soldiers during the two wars.

Uneasy Peace

Decades of easy peace
Time and tide drifted us apart.
You who shared our savage yesteryear,
Hold the highest place within my heart.

Past and present wrongs,
Humbled me, made me strong.
Cleansing flow of Exmouth air,
Calmed! I was taken to yesteryear.

Across the world's tempestuous seas,
Sunny Exmouth, Summer town at ease.
Shipwrecked addict. Exmouth is God here?
He was in those troubled times of yesteryear.

Above me, noiseless tumult, drifting cloud,
Blackened café, dark shadow like a shroud.
It groped the sky. Emanated a sense of fear,
Fighting youths remined me, of yesteryear.

We must love one another or decay and die,
75 years after the atomic Hiroshima's skies.
A melancholic note started to sing in my ear,
Uneasy peace! Since that savage yesteryear.

Was glad and thankful of those who died,
NHS workers who freely gave their lives.
Basked in the Sun, enjoyed my ice cream,
The whole day out was a magical dream.

Easter Gardens
Refrain by John M.C. Crum (1872–1958)

I have had my share of darkness I must confess,
Royal parade, Plymouth, a poetry of crocuses.
Rhythm of time, dead seeds, living underground,
Death defying spectacle, wonder all around.
Maybe the arrival of easter, speaks God is love,
Cremyll Street, wherever you are, look above.
Ferries, shopping, crowded cafes, mystery of life,
An easter garden speaks of faith, it'll be alright.

Now the green blade rises from the buried grain,
Wheat that in the dark earth many years has lain;
Love lives again, that with the dead has been:
Love is come again, like wheat that springs up green.

Grave clothes of winter, just black bare boughs,
Hear the thrush singing, dandelions and flowers.
Music of spring, singing, song rhapsody in green,
Sun in the sky starts to shine, Passiontide scene.
Easter gardens in England, no crown of thorns.
Pent up summer, on a wondrous holy week morn.
A draught of God, drunk from that elegant chalice,
Take off your shoes, holy ground, in God's palace

In the grave they laid Him, Love Whom we had slain,
Thinking that He'd never wake to life again,
Laid in the earth like grain that sleeps unseen:
Love is come again, like wheat that springs up green

A traveller from Ukraine, came dripping with blood,
Easter gardens destroyed, from Russia with love.
Priests are busy weeping, making a crown of thorns,
Graves haunted by ghosts; a ghastly world is born.
Myanmar, Yemen, people are puzzled, angry and bereft,
Jesus being crucified, Europe, world of war and death.
Few atheists! question, why is the divine gardener not here?
fortified by faith, will not be crushed! we will not fear!
Up He sprang at Easter, like the risen grain,
He that for three days in the grave had lain;

Up from the dead my risen Lord is seen:
Love is come again, like wheat that springs up green.

Eostra, pagan goddess, herald of new season spring,
See her running across the field, as summer begins.
Languid flowers magnolia! Beautiful! Pink and white,
Swansdown, silken, shining with their springly might.
New grass delivers richness, speaks of enchanted hope,
Elegant white goblets singing loudly, yes, we can cope.
Passiontide! The suffering God is here! Yes, He is love,
Easter garden's symphony, from the orchestra above.

When our hearts are saddened, grieving or in pain,
By Your touch You call us back to life again;
Fields of our hearts that dead and bare have been:
Love is come again, like wheat that springs up green.

There is a garden look within. Find it in your mind,
Water it daily with faith and love, not be spiritually blind.
Verities remain! Maybe we should plant what is true,
Be kind to ourselves, whatever you have been through,
Difficult choices! Wounded! Mental health! Desolation,
Fertilise your life with Easter faith in God's consolation.
The risen Christ is here, suffering in our turbulent world,
Cultivate the interior life, find comfort you are being held.

Easter season, ponder the meaning of death and resurrection.
Mystery of life! Pagan rituals! Ukraine! Christ's humble passion.
So many tragedies, funerals, issues out there lurking around,
With this suffering, we must search for joy which is to be found.
Dead looking seeds, become tasty food for us to thrive and live,
Christian truth! Christ died for us! That we may start to forgive.
Good Friday! Day of Crucifixion! A day seemingly we should be sad!
All these easter gardens have a different voice! Time to be glad.

When our hearts are saddened, grieving or in pain,
By Your touch You call us back to life again;
Fields of our hearts that dead and bare have been:
Love is come again, like wheat that springs up green.

Holy Russia

Farewell, my dear to all I love and hate,
Cold wind blowing from Russia, fickle fate.
Strange virus here, walking steadily abroad.
Ugly and noisy with its guns, shield, and sword,
Complacent, sleeping easily in our Western beds,
Holy Russia is stirring, missiles flying overhead.

Russia my dear is now a sepulchre of grievous crime,
Have mercy! on us Lord the potentate of time.
Ancient monster now broken out of his dark prison
Evil will not win, good has triumphed Christ is risen.
Silence from Patriarchs of Moscow, bells of war ring,
Wake up Holy Russia, before the mourners start to sing.

Ukraine my dear, has been visited by a thing of horror,
Like the fire that ranged down on Sodom and Gomorrah.
Despair is laying out a feast! Don't go, its food is poison.
Rise up above it! Remember it's the resurrection season.
Death august and royal, soldiers being taken to their tombs,
People of Ukraine fight! Get thee behind me spirit of gloom.

Guilt! Metaphysical! Moral! Political! Criminal! My dear
Holy Russian turned to evil. Realise our deepest fears.
Liberty! Sacred gift of Heaven! Time for new respect,
Treasure it! Don't misuse it! The judgement of neglect!
A tyrant mad with the eyes of war, we must now diminish,
Imitate the actions of a tiger! This war is not yet finished.

We are exhausted my dear, history has made us afraid,
Twenty first century four horsemen! A new strange age.
Must repent and believe, focus on noble concerns,
History is unfolding, apocalypse soon unless we learn.
Tumult and shouting will die, dictators will soon depart,
Stands the ancient sacrifice, of a humble and contrite heart.

CHUCK JURASTIK
AKA JOE VOSPER

STRING FOR BALLS

Brat III

English 8 yr old Math Torture Camps.

Show and do. Brains and ass humming. Work your wrist. Jesus is coming. I have to write the book to say I'm summing. I could knock her out, she's 76 and I'm a prime alter cyborg slumming. Sucking a straw off a dry clit. Sick of the Brits. Failing the cursive, saying the same. They never want an answer, just the fits. Win by wanting out of the game.
   Fuck you for the semolina. Fuck me for spelling it wrong and then right again. I couldn't have known the cook was illiterate, we got her in the papers though when we cracked her head open learning mesonics on the playground civics plain.
   Knee worn sack ware pumping against the chewing gum of yesteryear. Just another numb nuts slavering a dumb gum shield a whistle will never hear. Who never punched her out either. If this isn't my memory it wasn't yours neither.

All that's left is a cataract's contusion: A workaholics fear of how we live in communism. A choked apology for a life lived in any order-ism.

I've got sleep and let the world suss itself out What if it does it again!

You're right. You'll find us in your study group, talk enough we might reference you. Don't ever think we hurried. You had 14 weeks alone with Brian Adams and it wasn't enough for you! You're the only piss sick restriction never graduated to traffic light! You're a truant to your own Tyler Durdan who's forgotten one of the rules. Nothing to suffer left.

Lock yourself in. Only your mama will ever tell you it's necessary. Only your ego will ever tell you it's personal!

Taking a week off work on the pills chill. I'll be alright because my lawyer says I will I'm The Technocratics. I did great against The Pasadenas because I thought of this in time!

You live in darkness without suffering, a saint that never fell.
    Equidistant from every fake safety. You are the centre of hell.
    The only reason you can't sing is that you lie too well.
    You can't bank solely 'cos you can't make bail! You don't even float very well!

Couldn't bury me before they exposed Moore's law. I made the only back-up disc in the cloud boycott. I screamed life stinks at the tabaknackary and rode the October horse off!

I like hot dogs if they're free and they're not ripping off the IRS for 4.50. There's a little Sia Pokemon wombat in everybody. We're a 'shroom or Mogwai. Andy Warhol moved out from under your bed. Clean the sheets! And if you need to make it out of federalism, tether a Tomboy. You want to put me in a coma to listen to Madonna with me!

All any human being wants is to own every busted condom on the planet. I'm not over FED, I'm counter-borderism. Kicking over trellises drenched in elbow sweat. Of post temporal lefts around ears pinned forward. I roll like hey. I clock like co-reward. If I didn't knock you into next week, you'd be my very first would like to meet.

Why are you grabbing your crotch? You see a wasp? You want to slap it with a glove? Or put it off?
    I take care of myself like I'm a papyrus factory
    Shine in life to immortalise on the highest quality.
    A blemish is a blasphemy. Battle love!

It's musical statues but you just forgot the bones. I've forgotten the tones again. You're a sharp scrap who can't find the track on a soft ground. Lost in the woods 'cos I got grown and you think you're trim cos you got mowed down. This is a boring hobby. No-one shot JR and everyone I meet is a buddy Bobby!

I'll give you the veins from my wrist and your pussy can wear it as a negligee. You don't rock a night club. You came here to strip off and forgot your colouring pens. You brought your freak and you got a hurty, So don't get wordy! There's no flies on your grill cos you're a traffic cone empire, tip the weed. You're the piper! You forgot to say fuck you anyway!

I'm cosmopolitan like 'Oh fuck it, I'll fuck Forester!'
    I don't give a fuck. I want to stop writing please and call chorister. I'm so pinky I've got to know when you're going to grow a ring finger. I nibbled them all off and got teeth left! They're where I store my pigment, I'm English! It's not a bad thing to gulp alone, you know it doesn't mean you're from Arrakis! (Though?)

I only throw this spit around because I'm killing it! Art goes to the street when it knows there's no real air. Art goes to the stage when it can kick back a steel trap anywhere. Slink back take care. I want to see you bowling like you want to see me land a hyper-circus pin with my ass hair. I'm all the fun of the fair and all your friends crawled out of my nostril! The warriors did it! I shovelled an early midden and got sold as fudge.

Red painted feet under slave worn ankle socks. A dolphin nose surfing on my Wednesday cock! Give all your wet silk while I'm dancing through the rain drops!

Am I bodyist? Quickly. I want to wank off with a clear conscience.
    I hear an underlay under this Grandpa carpet. That could be you and me! Let's squirrel off before any these dribblers make a pail. Tails never fail. But do we want to sweep up afterwards?

Scared of what they are ignorant of. Ignorant of what they fear. Our higher level of pain for their deeper level of sanitation. Trope after trope. Year after year. Not a concern in common, but mutual invisibility. A shared freedom to avoid each other. An aversion to the office or to the street. At home in our horror of each other. Raise a stage and alight a visionary. Blinded by smoke we are together. Faded ticket stubs from a better time we never remember. Will you rally?

Risis

The 2008 banking crisis was just symptomatic of everything we've all been doing since the 90's: Moving things further onto the margin. Scaling up, again and again for a smaller returns every time, while we balanced the books with greater and greater diversification. Less and less brains controlling more and more markets.

My kind were the same. We wrenched the economy from a material one to a digital one, turning over one industry after another, music, TV, employment, finance. I was pitching in-game currency in 1999. We were 20 years ahead of the program and we knew every step of the play, but we were stepped on.

We planned a smooth transition, punctuated with a succession of mini revolutionary growth spurts. Technologisation in step with Leisure growth, in step with redundancy. A steady rate of manageable shock. Instead we got, retardation, distractions, glass ceilings and new monopolies. Stealth sophistication posing as greed, soft criminality and further ladder climbing. 20 years of division into soul masochism and gentrified horror.

Our political education wasn't the spectation of thousands of simulations on machines we all built, it was a puppet show of ever sillier, parody politicians. Somebody must have had the sense to realise the only level playing field was universal incredulity. At least, today, everybody knows they could do better than our leaders.

I'm still tired of it all but I've been tired all along. I am starting to worry, though, that the spiders are getting a little bit ginormous because we've all stopped pulling the flushes. I can't help asking myself if the, by now obvious, imminent enlightenment really needed all the starvation, despair, fury, persecution and utterly wasted time, and I'm not certain if I'm ready for another 20 years at this pace.

Tell me we're ready get started, finally.

Troglogate trust

This isn't when a good man goes to war. It's when a quartermaster starts to steal rations, and starts a million fashions. The devil's not trembling – he's laughing his ass off, at us, robbing our own banks and becoming bankers on the edges of our shrinking rocks and our siblings work for the saddest sluts in the universe.

The end of the world is not our invention. We're the privileged witnesses, the 7.7. We're the trollop of the polup, with our friend's foot on the rail, and the spade's for last christmas. Do the meeks for patricide and let's bust out the busts' busts. Trollogate the toprobate of the crust's tusks, re-aromate the gusts' pusseds, matronomate the musts muzzed. And get our junk late! A prives been prived but fussed has fussed.

You are a nob and you worked your bitch tail off – straight up genetic inheritance, but factually actually – you did it anyway.

Contracting at me because you have to authenticate a can of beans on the open seas.

I'm certain I can't lose my sanity. All of my supposed friends have always been certain I can survive my sanity. None of them ever suppose the world can survive our certainty thus! Big brother was never forever but it took a very deep scoop of the soup to get us together.

It's all for the people, it's a circus decathlon for the parade you never started that trampled everyone. Once people lose the last spine of the ration book to clean their teeth – they might speak!

The gravestone of our dreams says 'president' on one side and 'some cunt' on the other, and we look across it in dismay at our opposite mourner.

I can remember all of the days in my life when I wasn't robbed. Unfortunately though - I do!

Don't get between a skinny man and his stash, a crooked man and his bash, or a squeaky man and his cash!

You're too mad for me today. I'll catch you up tomorrow. If we can all say that to each other just maybe, we can mean it.

You can take it as a compliment and you can laugh, or you can take it as an insult and you can laugh.

We've got a hero complex or a bad conscience and that's a common interest monster.

If the government have a better record of everything I've ever done than I will ever have, why would I want my own shit back?

I'll make the money back my darlings, I promise ya. I'll clean my bits & pits up and cuddle ya!

This is the troglogate trust.

Vanya

There's been an alliance of the factions in my head: Why aren't I live? Why aren't I dead? What's a borrowed pot to a begged ladle when here to the front is as far as table to table. When everyone's screaming for your best self and they mean it, they're not about to begrudge you sleep, or cut off your fingers, as long as you give up the digits of your primary reason. March with the zombies or turn them into spidermen. Do you think the girthed bellies will take our off pets' collars when they still have their wellies, just because we concede our inferior intelligence? There's a definition of stupid and you're not helping, you're helpings.

I can kill myself standing still. And anything that's coming in, go home and tell. The manager's never in the building and you're not a real princess. The road back to serfdom is ritualized abuses and mutilation. If you're fully vaccinated, you have to live with this forever. You bit the wrong apple, stupid! The magic cooking pot is going to run out of oats soon and everything that's fabled gets Babled when it's finished. I'm a miss swing of a tadpole. I have an audience of precisely zero. I'm an asshole. I notice when they shift a great big stash of wet-wipes!

No point complaining that the calendar is all inked in. If it's objectionable, it is a symptom. If it's explanatory, it's a disease. I'm a Homo-toxin. Getting ready for chequered colour collar boxing. You remind me of the days when I was nearly sober, to think the cure for the mentally illnessed was to put us all together. Your dog's screaming. Your cat's pulling its fur out and your hamster is on the LAN ordering you knee bandages! Leroy's not good enough yet but he's still on the nearest rooftop, and we're freezing from the draft of our window cracks.

We've been hygiene punished. We're all gulagy.
    They'll have us crawling in shit, wiping it off our faces to look upon them, who have you full masked and meaty protecting them from us — the downwind shit heads fed from the hand of the nation of handless. I decide what to let them steal. I'm deciding right now. I hate ass fluff and I hate Manscape. That's all you need to know.

That's what drives reality. It's not the truth it's the summit where you walk away happy handed and fuck the world and having the power to say it. I'm passed fucking around. I loved it! Respect walks off the charge of being forever paid. I had my roach when the Cockrell called and you all smoked it. Sympathy? Are you hearing me porously? You brought the wrong perviousness to offer your services. Do you live on a Christmas tree?

I think there's egg on your face. A quiche shoe! Buried upside down in a flan to the laces they were careful to have left you. Don't you confuse love with respect. That was respect and I'd have to get angry if there wasn't any love left! I can be taller. I can be blinder. You can still be made to look down on the lot of me. What does it take to break the power of the few? Me to diminish. What happens when I do? It takes more of you! Co-living in internal conflict sharing only silent neurosis.

Getting it together means accepting everything that's special as particular and separating everything particular from what's special. We all need to practice dying in obscurity to emerge victorious. Nobody is supposed to recognise the final fight, but the participants who can never see it coming. It is a universal goal to live as we actually are. It is a universal necessity that we are instrumental to it. An ordered world is a lunatic asylum. Self-determined people live in it. History rhymes used to be a friend of mine to make Regis mean it. But used is used!

We rise up when we're falling so we'll stand at our full height when we're tombstoning. A private life is empty set rope climbing. If gravity is illusionary why is everybody swan diving? Sit down and shut up about the heat of the crust and the bugs surviving the dust. We saw the snorkel of your vortex. Don't fuss whether the sugar was floss or cane. Enjoy the fall and collect your Malaysian boyfriend. You racist fuck! If our true nature was couch potato then we've been chasing liars all along to keep us sane? All I need is one man to help me argue over wall colouring.

Night and day start together and we pay out only when we sleep. Back to data. See you later. The fate don't fete and the feint don't faint. The sprinkler sprinkler. Don't Deliveroo a doucher. Settle down. Give me back my space space fleets.

I'm going to travel the galaxy for hair clippings. I'm going to avoid nails. Treat everyone like lizard people and live by the scales. Demolition. What's a moll again? Moth to the heat of the troll aflame. Bye bye Ukraine! Nether Ishtar nor Icarus, shit to a Scythian. Some nigga bitch changed the nappy of the hero of all of them. Brucey bonuses and Bono balances Bona fide by Balko-Slavics. Seriously – what are we doing today? Buffering behind bogus bandwidths and shadow bans, blinded by bad signage and grappling with Greta taxes

Asylum, extradition, invitation or adoption too. Cos when you're half a world away, the other half's right behind you. Why am I so nasty to the Spanish? Viaje pappelles. Hiedi Klappe's dacha's got a Bruce Willis. All Saint's day needs a Dracula minute. I think I've confused myself that somebody else thinks they're somebody else and I'm scared that they've seen it. So obsessed with bribery, I wouldn't lend a library a paper for a cigarette.

I set my passion free so my mind will follow, not so I can wallow around in my puddle. I can still buy a baccy pack and choose to use the older one. In your face, neo-Orwellianism! I shimmy like the man on Britain's got talent with all the underpants and the contestants prevaricate. My heartache's like a truck company where every driver comes with a brick and no brake. But who over reacted? I founded Fagistan. What giant tosser deflected a meteor onto Chelyabinsk? My imaginary friend needed an imaginary friend. Here he is: Vanya Bydinerin, with a real health certificate, no vehicle and no cooking facilities.

Slaybells

We're two throws. I'm trebomiester and it's pokemon Go! What bit of me do you want at your show? 1, 2, Freddy's ready for you. Wear your bobbles. Held over a rail waiting for the right left pinkie nail.

Once it seemed strange that all the minerals were in layers. Once it seemed strange they weren't straight. It's not the size of the cake, it's how you frost it, and I'd throw it in everyone's face for a cut and a caustic.

You're not a man of the people anymore, you're lucky. Now move on before word gets around. Your legs are tied. You're magister of the mazed and the commissar of the hedged. You can go around but you can't get awryd!

What herb ain't a cock? What rain ain't a piss? I need to sit on a neon spike just to talk to myself, what other stabilisers do you want to impose?

The elite always find that something is forever always looking down on them and throwing them biscuits. Human beings have a way of self-righting. The universe is in crisis, it's not Planet Earth. Just look at the numbers of us needed!

Toad or an owl. Speaking part in the friezes, the distance between us. Saline drips through the self-cured around the rest of us. Pendulum, mated or divist. Nothing has been sacrificed. No-one was suicided. We finally celebrated our enemy's free ride without thanks or praise as they flew out of shouting range and we consumed what we needed. One over one is one again and the shame is all alone at the back of each mind indefeatist. The iron grip of two giant heads full of shit. If only one side would desist, the rest would march out of the warren apiece to repair this. A stupider misconception in ever decreasing absence of silliness, give up the ghost to the hilarious! The outside is simply the organellified. A skin, the border of a tide, the measure of a swell, the part of the movement by it's nature to stop, the inventor of the word for go – 'pop!'

This troll's life

The problem with elves: 'I'm not pissing in the lane – I'm repurposing the city as a treehouse.'

Elves and trolls on men - men on trolls and elves: Dousing on trails of fails. Googles gets the knuckles, we'll fake you for your nails. Grace and fury forged the hybrid master race.

Finite pence of shopper haulage, have to random hate on streets again, what random streets do they want me on? Hesitation, pixelation and delay, keeping my eyes off the ground and the sky. Days to rest and days until I suffer the healthy smelling. A half living half deserving the most of the shock of deliverance. You stale for the tailgate once in a lifetime but you bring vegetables, apologies and zero hand sanitation all the time on occasion, or on occasion all the time. I'm giving up the franchise for Trade Pick without a grade on him. I hate the flavour of the future and there ain't goona be a second helping. When did you wake up and fully effectivide zombid? A plummeted prom debutante on a draft of the early enwided, a pariah stain sick of the shadow of the still sycophantic a cell thick?

Queenjelly

Queenjelly. I know your true name. I cold read everybody! Pretty little elfin I spy. Professional paedophile in for a century. A kill for a cat's eye. She's having sex and he's biome studying. Same as same as it'll ever be, subrutalty. Absurdurgency. How do we save you? Cunt stick your head out! It is a zombie invasion. I'll knock 25 of you over before anyone has a chance to scream.

You're like 1972. I tasted all of it. I swallowed none of you!

The king of compliments and the prints of peace. Solve it with three bodies and tuppence. Wank stains – all of them and all of you. I'm looking for a few people today. Not a couple. And I love that line. Where does it go? Horlicks all round. Empty bucket of crushed ice and a tutor. What did I say?

If I can't translate by alphabetics, you're unnecessary!

When you cast your spells you invent another masonic title for me. I'm the perfect patsy culprit. I own nothing and I'm happy. Don't forget where natural justice lives: Lower dodgier, more adaptive. Why can't I live in a world where Luddites have the tech to find each other? Because I won't take the bunker bolt hole out of their way. Entitlement to our own little piece of Hawking radiation to homestead on, get to the pub in our mud and our muscles and do our citizenship against the wave of civilization ripping us off. You know like our newest neighbours, the Capitalists!

Rich wasn't wasting, they were just a fucking waste. Solving the wallpaper problem must have turned me into the paste, no-one's more susceptible to the out of context. It's only some Rizlas, but I'm full of takeaway so I know someone's dumped those greasy newspapers … but, that tear on that bar that I'm clinging by fingernails. There's gone. There's far gone. And there's still here! It's not sliding doors and it sure as fuck ain't Donkey Kong, it's a trampoline of pricks, and you're the door that's got to smack my ass on the way out. Our narrative is the funeral march of the people we want to hunt down. I love it. Do me now!

College shit! If you gave him his bollocks back he'd abolish it! I'm definitely doctor zero. It was the silent elections. Our battle's beefier than Bodied 30 if we wrote the other 28! I've got a feeling I'll never find the bottomless bottle. You can have me today! I've got the ego problem. When's your karma going to cure it? I must be a machine. I'm going to campaign for my rights. I finally found a bigger complaint than being white!

I ain't superstitious. I don't need a mythology to get things twisted. Fuck shopping. I just want a knuckleduster with a really good face cover.

You hate everything about metal except denim!

A new word for you: Trim. Hurl if you want, throw if you're dim.

Everyone else is some obscure abolitionist Everyone's compromised by what those pricks wanted.

If we were transgendered pan-dimensional knicker twists. Then we could stop and see that we're all just cunts.

If speak for yourself was all you came here to say. Stay home the next time! I've got your people in my palm and the wax is your pant stains Rashed or not, don't egg me on again. That's fighting talk. It's a pity it's in my language. I don't want to be binary. I'm already walk don't walk! Tell me you came here with one blister to bust but you crucified the whole audience.

Cancel Culture. What's this access thing? The fused conwhosed?

Fix both sides of the fight, play three at once and feed us pervert bingo callers. Whiter than me, I can't even genuflect, sorry about the last time but you're making me crescent shaped. I'd choke myself but it feels selfish to breath you in! It's like you're me being honest about what I really like! Down! … and less jokes about Manscape!

Glaze consortiumist, bagel corporatist. Get in bed with anyone. You make the breakfast, I ain't eating your shit. I'll eat the holes though! Wednesday's that kid you want to adopt. gets you out weekends thrashing the crop. Start them today and never land from the chop. The indulgence of poverty: Eating, fucking and honesty.

I'm the best writer there ever was. And never needed to be.

All I need in life is a self-installing length of pipe, a hard drive and a painted drain. I can always find myself and be lost in their world whenever they demand me. Survival is a newspaper, a pay day a day late and a trip to B&Q, keep funding education. Live, let live and let them name the price. It never pays.

Start making promises you can't keep. You can keep most of them and they're not going to matter anyway. Once we add up all the will, it's poorest pocket in infinity and who's been playing with you lately? Cureds always healthy and ills as well.

The old west was the invasion of space won by the best fake rickets, and your whole audience is Earthling except for their birth certificates. Imprisoned with people I owe money to. I can't get out to spread the love as if that would get me more apartment space.

Everyone's surname is the seventh recurring.

Why are you pretending to be me?
    How am I pretending to be you?
    We can do this all night, but the second you leave, you're going to be pulled into the back of a van.
    But the second I get pulled into that van, you've lost your ride!
    A man falls into a hole … I'm going bite off one of my legs and prove that a spider and lizard against a monkey isn't a fair fight. Too many eyes cannot scare me a little bit, rolling your tongue at me while I skate on my spit. I stop and I search vegans and lentils. Making a friend this year proved you're not friendly or environmental. So take your blame game to your bribed ass. Chase your tail.

Fuck outdoors if it don't look like rape. Every good house was built on grape. Get your pace up. Scream out of this place. Don't be strutting if your noting nothing. Knittings done by the bitch with her heel trained! We're all the result of an illegal sale of a dog without a boy with a skateboard or a skateboard a without a dog and a lead, and the sale of a planet where a skateboard can't jerk itself off! So we concede abide and abide concede. Oh dear. True colours. I wish they'd just kill me!

JACKIE WACHA

SIMPLE REFLECTIONS

Within these Walls No Resting Place (A Reflection on Ford Park Cemetery)

Dark winter nights and the gates close by four o'clock.
Within these walls, redwing arrive to feed until the berries are gone.
Flocks of tits, long tailed, and blue, converge in the trees,
-and hidden among them, the smallest of all, *regulus regulus*, a goldcrest,
    greyish green with a black and yellow stripe, picking insects between
    pine needles.
Pied wagtails, their tails 'a shiver', rest on an anchor, the seafarer's
    symbol of hope.
Should the weather turn for the worse, a snipe might suddenly abandon
    its hiding in the thickets.

As the days lengthen the early daffodils and primroses join the carpet of
    grasses.
Bluebells and wild garlic follow, standing guard at the western boundary
    like colourfully scented troops.
And later still, white, green and cool pink umbellifer line the paths, their
    aroma attracting insects and keeping the best company on your
    walk.
The song of new beginnings sung by chaffinch, you hear them well
    before you see them, their patterned plumage blending and merging
    with the colours on the ground.
Song thrush, and red breasted robins join the spring chorus.
Roused by a sudden movement, the butterflies perched on the bushes
    and on the heads of stone angels take flight in a myriad of colour –
Brimstone and holly blue flutter away.
Up in the trees - birch, beech, cedar, ash or oak a *streptopelia turtur*, a
    dainty turtle dove gently purrs, its feathers mottled with chestnut
    and black, breaking its long journey to breeding grounds far away.

As the sun shines brighter and warmer, the ox-eye daises host beetles of
    shimmering metallic green,
and in the grasses by the monkey puzzle tree, the bush cricket is
    expertly camouflaged, but follow that loud and insistent sound as it
    rubs its forewings together, and you will find it.
Everywhere there are moths, bees and hoverflies, forever busy.
Joining them in mutual industry, the striking and brightly coloured
    common blue butterfly, and occasionally, the distinctive black and
    white wings of the marble white, perched on the yellow flowerheads
    of the ragwort and the fluffy wind-borne seeds of the creeping
    thistle
Within these walls there is no resting place.

The summer is alive with squirrels, and wood mice, and ladybirds and
    bats and spiders and snails
Once, a hedgehog passed by, a rare sight.
Flying to and fro between the cemetery and the park - the
    sparrowhawk, the kestrel, the swallow, the swift, the crow and the
    magpie
 – and most surprising- ring necked parakeets with their bright green
    plumage and distinctive call.

Now the seasons come full circle and more seasonal visitors fly in – on
    their way to warmer climes.
There are enough berries to feed them on their way -holly, and
    hawthorn in abundance.
Grey squirrels store acorns from the many oak trees, burying them as
    the autumn leaves begin to fall.

Rosa Louise McCauley Parks

Rosa Louise McCauley Parks was tired of having to sit in the
    coloured section of the bus
tired of having to give up her seat when a white person demanded it
tired of being denied a seat that she had paid for
tired of being a second-class citizen

Rosa Louise McCauley Parks was tired of the Ku Klux Klan
    marching down her street
tired of black men hanging from trees like strange fruit
tired of cases like the Scotsboro boys being falsely accused of rape
tired of instances where black women like Recy Taylor were gang-raped
she was tired of the injustice when the brutal white murderers of 14-
    year-old Emmet Till were acquitted
tired of the killing of three innocent young black men by the police in
    the Algiers Motel incident

Rosa Louise McCauley Parks was tired of the racism and the
    segregation
tired of not knowing what rights she had as a citizen and a human being
tired of the black world and the white world
tired of being mistreated
tired of giving in, of complying with the treatment
her patience had run out and she could endure it no longer.

So **Rosa Louise McCauley Parks** refused to give up her seat on a
    bus.
She helped to change the course of history.

The Mud

I asked him to tell me, the story of the war
I asked him once, I asked him twice, I asked again once more
He shook his head, as he had done for many a year to date
He looked so old, so frail and lined, I feared I was too late
For forty years his silence held, my pleadings did not sway
I knew that short the memory, would soon some vile trick play
Then one day, he said at last: 'There was a lot of mud!'

I urged him on to speak his mind, yet knew to hold my tongue
He looked so weary and so sad, as shrunken hands he wrung
His voice was soft, his tone was low
Yet every word was strong and slow
'The wet was wet, with rain and rain
The land it drowned, in the vast plain,
And the world became a sucking bog
Full of greed, a hungry hog
Slippery and thick, treacherous and dense
We waded in a swamp that made little sense
We crept and we crawled and we burrowed chest deep
And clambered over bodies that lay in great heaps'

'We slept in the mud, covered deeply in grime
It swallowed and choked, with no rhythm nor rhyme
It weighted our clothing from head down to foot
It filled every cavity, mouth, ear, pants and boot
For all kinds of sickness, our skin played the host
You were lucky to lose a leg, if a leg was all you lost
And the itching and the biting and scratching from the lice
And the gnawing and the feasting from the rats and the mice
And the fat flies in droves swarming in a haze
Devouring the dead, as blankly they gazed
And the stench in the trench, so putrid and foul,
It brought on the madness, it loosened your bowel
And the banging and the firing of artillery shell

Bombardment and barrage, sounding the knell
Mustard gas consuming the throat and the lung
Blistering the skin, burning mouth, face and tongue
Then the Captains whistle to 'go over the top'
Over fallen comrades we nimbly must hop
During the night, from the mud dug them out
With spades and hands and sticks that were stout

Then the skies relented and for a little while
The sun returned with its warming smile
We drained trenches, filled sandbags, mined new ones too
Polished bayonets, read letters and remembered those who
Were crying and waiting and hoping and praying
That those whom they loved would soon be returning

We fought in the mud and we died in the mud
That was vomit, and urine, and corpses and blood
They were nameless bodies and bodiless names
Willing players of this great war game
Now side by side at Menin Gate
Too young, too soon, to die, too late
We remember the thousands in statuary and stone
Yet hundreds more will never be known
And marble and granite adorn the green for miles
So if I say nought, and just linger here awhile
Tis' to look at the field of poppies that grow blood red
And remember, remember my friends that are dead.

I Remember (An Elephant's Reflection)

I remember when the clouds did not come and the rains failed
Shimmering waves of windless heat rising in the stillness and the pain of
    thirst
The waterholes, long dried and ridged with cracks, the earth seemed
    cursed
The never-ending march over the savannah, slow, silent dreary and bleak
The hunger and the weariness, that left us so weak
The love, care and compassion, as we marched side to side
Tenderly comforting and cajoling as one by one we died
I remember my dear brother, I remember my beloved mother

I remember the gathering, once one hundred strong and counting
Through the long difficult years, now but twenty-five remain
Our numbers, old and young, slowly but surely on the wane
I remember the Matriarchs, leading us as one, keeping the family
The courtships, the rituals, games in waterholes, contented and free
The joy and delight, when the calf was conceived
The long wait, the anxious months, before the new-born was received,
I remember the deep affection, as I pause in quiet reflection

I remember when the villages moved closer into the savannah
Our world gradually diminished and eroded in the noonday heat
Sweet grasses uprooted to plant things we could not eat
Trees with delicious bark felled and disappeared
And so in search of food we went to the villages that appeared
And were greeted as intruders in our own land
Hounded harassed and chased by the human hand
For other food we had searched in vain, so were forced to eat their
    sugarcane

I remember the crack that rent the air by the watering hole
And the thunder beneath our panicked feet as we fled from sudden danger
Brought into the savannah by a murderous unknown stranger
And then at last we stopped to the realisation that we had lost another
Desolate, we returned to find my dearest brother

A gaping hole where his tusks had been that morning
I remember the grieving, the sorrow and the mourning
There was nothing to be said to the bones of the dead

I remember the savannah, when the rains finally came
The pleasing aroma of wet earth as it absorbed these life-giving gifts,
And beyond, to the mountains, the ridges and the rifts
The music of the stream babbling its happy song
The awakening of creatures that had waited for so long
The shoots of tender leaves on the acacia tree
The carpet of sweet grasses spreading far wide and free
I remember it all as my eyes, my eyes close to sleep their last.

The Child Soldier

He marched his boots in my direction
I wondered should I cross the road
I hesitated. It was too late.
He would know that I was afraid. Afraid of him.

I glanced at him
Trying desperately to appear casual and willing myself
To breathe normally
I did not want to meet his eyes, in case he spoke to me.

On he came towards me
I was forced to stop
My bladder protested
I felt the cold night breeze on my face and in my heart
It was the hour after the light and before the dark
I looked for sympathising faces and witnesses on either side of the street
But there was no one in sight.
I was alone. With him.

My eyes strayed, out of control
He was two feet away
I was taller than him
his boots, a couple of sizes too big
His face, no more than thirteen or fourteen
Too young to understand the devastation
The pain and grief that his metal stick could bring
The breath was squeezed out of my lungs

I reached into my pocket
And took out my identity card
Made to offer it to him
My hand shook. He strode past
His heavy boots kicking up the dust
His uniform, hanging off his thin shoulders

He had not seen me
Or he did not care.

I sighed with relief
Then saw him turn, stop, and come back towards me
reach into his pocket
His deadly stick now swinging from side to side
'Have you got a light?' he said, holding out a cigarette
I felt a warm wet rush down my trousers
It filled my shoes and pooled at my feet
I shook my head in shame.

Waiting for the Rain

The season was right as we knew from past years
In the back of our minds lay unspoken fears
We prepared the seeds, tilled the land, resolute, resilient
We worked hard and long, determined, diligent
The vultures flew and circled wide and high
As we looked up at the cloudless sky
Knowing it will soon rain

We dug a little more, planted a few more seeds, the rain was late
People sat in circles, quiet discussion and debate
There was no wind, just the sun that beat down
On our backs, as we looked at each other with worried frowns
We asked the medicine man, but he didn't know why
The sun was so hot and no rain fell from the sky
We waited and hoped for the rain

We prayed to the rain God, we beseeched and pleaded
Was it a goat or sheep, a sacrifice that was needed?
Our animals were losing the meat from their bones
Without water, or grass, anxious grumblings and groans
We raided the granary stores for last years crop
But it was soon gone, a temporary prop
And still we waited for the rain

There was nothing to feed the children, not even with lies
As they looked at us with hungry, accusing eyes
At first they cried, then they were silent,
Their fleshless arms and legs deformed and bent
The dusty soil was parched, as waves of heat
Rose from the ground and burned our feet
We cried and prayed for the rain

A man came to our village, from Somalia, he said
'I'm looking for the rain, all my people are dead!'
Another came, from the Ethiopian Mountains
He was thin and thirsty –'I'm looking for the rains!'
'We have not seen the rains for three long years
Everything is dry here, even our tears!'
We, too, are waiting for the rain.

The bones of our animals bleached in the sun
The wells were empty, there was nowhere to run
We buried our children in shallow graves or caves
The arid soil too hard to dig, unrelenting heatwaves
The seasons had changed, we did not know why
All we could do was weep and cry
We waited for the rain that never came again.

A Walk by the Nile

Come with me down to the water's edge
by the riverside
see the dragonflies
the African sun sparkling on the Nile
I catch a Nile Perch - fish for our supper
let us stay until the sun has set
and the hippo has gone to feed
see the moon reflected on the water
do not fear that old crocodile
we need only stay away from his nest
dip your toes into the cool water
hold my steadying hand
then sit with me on the fine clean sand
and I will anchor you

come with me up to the top of the hill
in the early dawn
when the dew sits heavy on unopened buds
and the smell of fresh grass fills your senses
like heady wine
in that magic hour
the sky is tinged with red, and the sun is rising just over the horizon
see the neat rows of sunflower fields down below
stretch your arms and reach out to touch the sky
the air is sharp and crisp
see the world come alive, the dawning of a new day
hear the crickets sing their song
the early birds join the harmony
sing with them, it is only I who hear
and I will never judge you
If you should stumble, I will catch you
put my steadying hand upon your back

come with me in the evening gloom
watch the moon come into her own
as the light fades
a thousand myriad stars stake their place in the sky
the creatures beneath your feet
scurry off to hunt or feed their young
light reflects on the water and the world is at peace
clear your mind of all thought
breathe deeply and freely
inhale the night scent of the evening primrose
Let the peace of the night flow through your veins
Reach out to me, share the moment
And I will hold you in my heart for all time.

My Last Farewell

Strange into the silence, my daughter's shrill and strident wail,
Against cold walls of stone and stone her helpless arms flail
Painted glass, of noble peoples, shimmer restlessly to and fro
Shuffling feet, shifting shoulders, uncertain in the face of woe
Marked out in trough and furrow, anguish lines her dear face so!
My sister weeps in sorrow, for what, I do not know!

At a box of polished mahogany, my dearest grandson stood
'Wake up Nana, wake up now, I promise to be good!
I do not like this game Nana, it makes my mummy sad!'
And if Nana won't wake up now, I'm sorry if I was bad!'
A man I think I recognise takes the boy to his dad
'It's hard on kids,' I hear him say, 'look after your little lad!'

And to the crowd he says again, 'It's time to say farewell!'
They file past, heads bowed and low, as they listen to the knell
And then their voices rise and swell, singing their parting song
The dirges are my favourite hymns, echoes rebound loud and long
And through it all, my son subdued, trying, failing to be strong
Bewildered and lost, alone and forlorn, oblivious to the chanting throng.

I look inside the silk lined box, a strange familiar sight
Who is that woman, cold marble skin, so pale in the harsh light?
I think I've known her all my life, but cannot recall just where
She's shrunk somehow, pitiful and still, silently lying there
Her powdered face, emotionless, stripped of any care
I see my daughter tender, gentle, sadly stroke her hair.

LIZ WRIGHT

KINTSUGI

The bowl shattered as it hit the floor when my arm, in anger brushed against it. For nearly fifty years it had rested in serene tranquillity on the shelves of four kitchens. It had survived house moves, withstood the tumble of rambunctious toddlers and storming teenagers, only to become victim of an old lady's tantrum.

"It's our Golden Wedding! Something to celebrate with friends and family for Christ's sake!" I shrieked.

"Why have all that fuss? Surely it should be a private occasion for the two people involved, not an excuse for a party?" he responded.

On and on it went; the same things said over and over till I swept out of the room, blinded by scalding tears.

Later, gathering up the shards of porcelain I reflected on the symbolism of the bowl's fractures and the spider's web of cracks in the glaze. Did they represent the fissures of our marriage? Was I the web's spider or its victim fly? Sorrowfully I tried to piece it together, but it was impossible.

Such a thing of beauty, our favourite wedding present. John had been working for the Foreign Office in Tokyo, with me as his secretary, until it turned into a less professional relationship. We were married in the Spring, under a cloudless kingfisher sky, beneath a cascade of cherry blossom. A day of perfect joy. The bowl was made by our dear friend Akio Tanaka, long before he became one of Japan's most celebrated potters. Looking at its remains now, there is still the soft silvery grey of the cherry tree's bark shot with amber, the inside the turquoise of the sky with a faint glow of rose.

Apart from Christmas and birthday cards, we were no longer in touch with Akio, but he might still be able to help. Maybe create a copy? John and I were enduring an uncomfortable silence, so I didn't tell him of my plan, fearing ridicule, more harsh words. I rang the last number I had for the old craftsman. His daughter Suzuki answered.

"I am living here now," she announced. "Father is in care home. Very nice place. He love to speak with you. I give you number, but not to ring at these times when he eat or have treatment." A lengthy timetable followed.

Akio did love to speak with me, his English still perfect. The care home staff even set up a Facetime link for us. I could see that his once strong, supple hands were gnarled and twisted like the branches of the trees he reflected so beautifully in his work. So he could not make another bowl like the first, but spoke gently with me of another way.

"In our culture, if a thing of great beauty is broken or cracked, we do not throw it away. Instead, we repair it with liquid gold. It seeps into the cracks and the layers of chipped glaze. And the object becomes even more lovely.

"You see," he continued. "We are all imperfect, flawed human beings. Sometimes we have a veneer like the glaze on a bowl, which hides our faults. Kintsugi lets the cracks show, filling them with the gold of human kindness.

"I will give you the number of my old pupil, Haru, living in London. His name means born in the spring sunshine. This is a good omen for you, I think. But now I must sleep."

We said our goodbyes, with hopes to meet again.

The next day I rang Haru. He was not prepared to mend our bowl. Instead, he insisted that this task be completed by me, under his close supervision. It took two long, difficult days of intense concentration. But I embraced every break, flaw and crack in the bowl, filling them with pure liquid gold, which hardened to create wandering tendrils of delicate beauty.

I was filling the kettle for our morning tea when I heard John's cautious steps entering the kitchen. They stopped as he gasped at the sight of the symbol of our enduring love with its many flaws and cracks, resting in its usual place on the kitchen counter.

In my hands, he placed a bundle of hand-made Golden Wedding invitations.

"Thank you, my darling," he murmured. "I daresay there will be more cracks before we're done. And more gold to fill them."

We arrived at Lima Airport around 11.30pm. Susie's appetite for spontaneity meant not having booked anywhere to stay, so we were immediately the prey of eager touts, before succumbing to the seemingly least rapacious, a motherly looking soul called Carmen. Having informed us that *The Senorial* hotel, recommended by a friend of Susie's, was closed, Carmen hailed a taxi which whisked us off to the *Hotel Eiffel*. Double commission for Carmen then. This establishment did not live up to its elevated title, but it was clean and we even had a surfboard in our room for company. And a very welcome hot shower, followed by the bliss of a good night's sleep.

Unlike this self-confessed Slut of this Parish, accustomed to living out of a rucksack, Susie had unpacked. I was awoken by a clanking sound and the sight of her belongings arranged on her bed. I'd been too tired to pay any attention the previous night but was now intrigued by a large Nescafe tin.

"Why have you brought coffee, Susie? They do have it in South America, you know. Besides, I thought you weren't that fussed on it."

"Er ... well ... it's not coffee. It's me mam. Half of her anyway."

"Bloody hell! You mean you've carted a tin full of grey powder all the way from Newcastle to South America! I'm surprised you haven't got us arrested!"

A guilty self-realisation of gross insensitivity controlled a further outburst.

"It was well hidden. You always said I was good at packing."

Bella, Susie's mum, had passed away two years previously. She'd been an amazing woman, one of sixteen kids brought up in a three bedroomed terraced house in the fishing village of Cullercoats, her own mother carried out of the washhouse for every birth. Even the twins. Creels for cradles. In later life, the front door of her council flat in the street where Susie and I had been friends since we were toddlers, was always open. You could tell Bella things you couldn't tell your own mam, she'd seen it all. Broken heads, busted bikes, broken hearts; she'd have a go at fixing them. I think I'd loved her almost as much as Susie had. And still did.

"Sorry bonny lass. Shouldn't have snapped at you like that. Just a bit surprised that's all. And wondering what you're planning on doing with her?"

"I want her to be with Joe, Cath. He was the love of her life. She never really got over him dying so young like that, so far away from home and the folk he loved. The rest of her is under the cherry tree in my garden, but at least some of her should be with him."

I knew the story of Bella's first marriage, aged seventeen, to a handsome merchant seaman whose photo remained by her bedside throughout her second marriage to Susie's father. Bella was seven months pregnant with her eldest son, wee Joe, when she received the news of her husband's death from septicaemia onboard ship. War had broken out by then, she couldn't remember receiving any paperwork and was too preoccupied with grief and bringing a bairn into the world to take much in. Especially with nowt much to live on. But she remembered being told he'd been buried in an English Cemetery in South America. The love they'd shared never had the chance to become tarnished by years of hardship and the clash of two strong personalities, which were features of her second marriage to Susie's dad.

"You know, when she was dying, she could hardly breathe, with the emphysema and all that. But towards the end she kept on saying his name. Then the night before ... you know ... she said "Ancon, that's where he is. I found out Ancon is just outside Lima. Looked it up in my world atlas. So that's why I wanted to start out here."

"Did you check with the Merchant Seamen's' records, pet?" I gently enquired, knowing that this was unlikely- it just wasn't the way Susie did things. It's what makes us such good travelling companions – her amazing optimistic spontaneity combined with my sceptical caution. Give or take a few tense moments over the years.

"No need to complicate things" with a toss of long blonde hair. "We've just got to find out how to get there. You can speak Spanish, can't you?"

In preparation for our ten-week adventure through Peru, Bolivia and Chile, I had been absorbed in BBC's *Suenos* Spanish course for precisely two weeks. Hardly fluent. Susie had flicked through a phrase book on the plane and knew how to request *una cerveza*.

We treated ourselves to a couple of nights in *The Senorial* (which was of course open) and settled in, room overlooking a garden, doves cooing, no surfboard. The urbane English-speaking proprietor, on hearing of our mission, advised us on transport to Ancon, 40 kilometres away, surmising from our well used travel gear that it wouldn't be by taxi.

"This will not be easy," he added ominously.

"Oh, he's just underestimating us because we're two old broads," Susie breezed.

Into Lima Centro in a *collectivo*, with the conductor dangling from the bus shouting his fares. Still dozy we wandered round the old colonial centre, admiring the grandiose government building with its toy town guards. Breakfast sustained us till evening when, after a copious meal of fresh fish, rice, salad, yucca and fresh pineapple juice, we were ready for a jet lag early night. However, heading for the bus stop, our attention was seized by a solemn procession, its participants clad in purple robes with white girdles. They were following a glittering shrine, watched by throngs of the faithful, all ages from tiny, huge-eyed *niños* to dignified elders. With a sombre rhythm, a band measured the steps of an incense swinging priest.

"*¿Que pasa?*" I inquired of an older woman who had approvingly patted my rucksack, firmly clutched to my front to ward off pickpockets. She smiled in apparent delight at my lame Spanish.

"*Esta la fiesta de Los Milagros del Senor de Nazarenes.*"

"JC to you and me," whispered Susie, neither of us believers, bewitched by the spectacle nonetheless. We perched on a ledge by the church door, entranced by the mosaic of flower petals within, its delicate creation contrasting with the purple and white balloons on the altar and the ends of pews.

The procession entered the cathedral, accompanied now by joyous singing, cheers, fireworks and balloons floating off into the night sky. The air was sweet with the scent of leftover incense as we struggled to the bus, through the dispersing crowd and sellers of tawdry souvenirs.

"What a welcome," breathed Susie as we sank gratefully into our beds. And I agreed.

The next morning, fortified by another delicious breakfast and the warmth of our introduction to Peru, we caught the *collectivo* to the bus station, the same acrobatic conductor greeting the *señoras* like old friends.

It took more than an hour to find the stop for Ancon. This was admittedly because of confusion over the Spanish verb for "to take or catch". Unbeknown to me, *coger* has an unfortunate colloquial meaning in

South American Spanish. Asking where we could copulate with a bus in Ancon resulted in uncontrolled mirth from the local youths, as well as enthusiastic alternative offers, before they gleefully helped us onto the right transport.

We drove north for over an hour past colourful markets, a sprawl of overcrowded shanties, half-naked children playing in the dirt. Finally, a bleak, litter strewn highway led us to Ancon by midday.

The town was a pleasant surprise- a nucleus of beautiful old colonial houses and small hotels which we later learned were relics of Ancon's heyday as a deluxe beach resort in the late nineteenth century. There was a handful of newer hotels on the seafront and the fishing port and pavement cafes gave the place a continental feel. Hopeful, hungry pelicans patrolled the harbour awaiting the catch, while we drank much needed coffees.

The cemetery seemed the best place to start. Our waiter seemed friendly but spoke no English and even my basic Spanish was deserting me after the bus station fiasco. Failing to remember the word for graveyard, I resorted to "*¿Donde estan los muertos?*" The waiter's smile faded at the prospect of two crazy, middle aged English women Zombie hunting amongst his dearly beloved, but directed us to a bleak, walled enclosure on the outskirts of town, a gruelling uphill walk in the baking sun.

We combed the neglected, arid cemetery searching the stones for Joseph William Charlton. Many of the markers were broken, many illegible and of course, most were in Spanish. There was one rickety wooden cross with the stark words "John Henderson Mariner" but no other English names.

After a weary trudge down the hill, Susie's ebullience diminished by the depressing experience, we came to a huge building on the seafront bearing the title "Municipio". Surely the town hall would have records of burials? Although the staff were really helpful, they spoke very little English, but we managed to get directed to the Hatches, Matches and Dispatches department. By now Susie was close to tears and my head was spinning with the effort of trying to speak and understand Spanish. However, pulling out a notebook, writing "1939" and "Joseph William Charlton" together with a great deal of sign language, produced the register of deaths for that year.

The names of six English sailors were recorded but his was not one of them. There was some talk that his death may have been registered elsewhere, particularly if he had died in hospital. Seeing Susie's distress, an elderly employee volunteered to drive us back to the cemetery to show us where Joe's countrymen were interred, just in case there had been an administrative error and there was some sign he was there. We again encountered John Henderson, the other graves unmarked, leaving us guessing as to whether this was Bella's beloved Joe's resting place, or not.

Susie decided against leaving her mam in this desolate spot – "She wouldn't like it" – we took some photos, said thank you to our kind, concerned driver and caught (*tomar* this time) the bus back to Lima, the grim, poverty stricken tin shacks of the favelas on its outskirts adding to our pensive mood.

"Let's have an ice cream to cheer ourselves up" Susie announced on reaching the Bus Station. The same group of youths we had unwittingly entertained in what seemed like days ago, were hanging around the *helado* kiosk.

"*Dos helados, por favor.*" As the ice cream seller began to spoon his wares into cardboard cups, Susie and I indicated with explicit mobile hand gestures our preference for cones. Realising the delighted effect on our avid audience, we looked at each other in mock dismay before, licking our ice creams with exaggerated lasciviousness, we sauntered out of the building, laughing as we went.

Postscript

Two years later I received a phone call from Susie who was travelling solo in South America.

"I've found him," she declared. "They're together at last."

I knew at once what she meant, because on returning from our first trip we'd consulted the Merchant Seaman Records in Britain. That's where we discovered that Joe Charlton was indeed buried in Ancon, not in Peru but in Panama, after being taken ill as his ship went through the Panama Canal.

Arms folded, supporting a copious bosom, Jemima leant over the shop's wooden counter and gave her customer a hard, uncompromising glare.

"You'll pay the two shillings we agreed, Daffydd Griffiths or you'll see me the other side of this counter to shake it out of you. That's nearly a new pair of boots you've got there, so none of your cheating ways. And it's no use looking over my shoulder for Llewellyn. He's gone to find out what that noise was. Sounded like it came from the fort, it did."

Griffiths quailed under the impact of the formidable figure, edging towards the door of the cobbler's shop, boots under his arm. He'd hoped to do business with Jemima's husband, a much more flexible prospect when it came to payment.

"Well, I was just going to find out myself. There's a right old hullabaloo going on outside. Talk of French warships sailing into the bay by Lower Town. The cannon's fired from the fort to sound the alarm. You can see the flame against the night sky, you can. Llewellyn should be back soon with more news. I'll look after the shop for you if you want to go look."

"Take my mind off the two shillings, you mean. But yes, I will do that. Can't trust the men round here to do anything, soused as they are on smuggled brandy."

Griffiths peered out into the street.

"Hush, woman. There's the militias assembling outside The Royal Oak. They might hear you. We don't want them to know what we found on that shipwreck, do we? They'll only take more than their share."

Wrapping her scarlet, woollen shawl against the chill February wind, Jemima joined the shabby figure at the door, lowering her booming voice to a whisper.

"That's the truth you're telling for once, Daffydd. It's rogues they are. We don't want them to find the liquor and victuals stashed out at Trehowel alongside Farmer Williams' good hams and cheeses, ready for Myfanwy's wedding. It's a great send-off he'll be giving her. A fine feast for the whole town", smacking her lips in anticipation.

"Ah, here's Llewellyn, look you. I'll be back with more news shortly". Daffydd weaselled swiftly past Jemima's imposing bulk, before losing himself in the gathering crowds.

"Drat the man, he's done it again. I'll have his hide for riding boots when I catch up with him" Jemima addressed her husband.

"He's a sly one to be sure, but we'll catch him later. Great excitement and perturbation out there, cariad. Boney's warships have stuck their noses into Fishguard Bay, but they've been seen off by the canon fire. Retreating westwards. That's the last we'll see of them, I'll be thinking."

"Well, I'm thinking they won't give up that easily. How do we know they haven't found somewhere to land?"

"Some of our boys are marching up to the headland to have a look. They'll call for reinforcements if needs be."

Later, the men gathered in The Royal Oak to hear the outcome from the bedraggled band of wind-blasted, rain-soaked men returning from their mission. The reluctant leader of the group told of how, as they'd arrived at Carregwastad Point, they had seen two ships sailing away near Llanwnda beach. Relieved and ready for their dinner and bed, they were returning by way of Trehowel Farm a couple of miles inland, when they heard voices in a strange tongue. Fortunately, the clank of metal drowned out their own murmurings. Diving into the bushes they could just make out, in the shifting shadows, a group of figures. Some toted rifles, some carried barrels on their shoulders. They were making their way into the sprawl of farm buildings at Trehowel, where others greeted them with raucous shouts.

"The noise we heard wasn't just the rifles; some of them had broken leg irons. Shackled they were, freed prisoners I suspect. It's desperate those Frenchies must be, if that's all they have for an invading force. Mind you, there were hundreds of them, and I reckon it was gunpowder in those barrels by the smell, so too much for us this night. I daresay we'll call on Lord Cawder in the morning for more men and rifles and we'll surprise them. What they've done with Farmer Williams and his good woman I don't know."

"Don't you worry about Mr and Mrs Williams," boomed a voice from the back of the room. "They've gone to visit Myfanwy's betrothed and his family at St David's. Though why she couldn't marry a Fishguard boy I don't know."

Scandalised to see a woman in the inn, some of the men looked at Llewellyn Nicholas in mute appeal. He in turn looked down at his perfectly cobbled boots, before with what dignity he could muster, rising and following Jemima home.

The next day the whole of Fishguard had heard the news of the invasion and turned out to watch Lord Cawder muster the militia, ready to march behind it with whatever weapons they could find or fashion. Jemima strode at the head of hundreds of women, all proudly dressed in their best red shawls and black stove-pipe hats. Their menfolk had tried to insist they stay at home out of danger's way, but, wary of the pitchfork she was wielding, were no match for Jemima and her battalion.

Waves of nervous tension rippled through the ranks, aware of the report of the great number of vicious armed ex-convicts at the farm, together with the uncomfortable realisation that they could be outnumbered. However, encouraged by the women, they marched towards Trehowel, their singing blending with the strident cries of their wives, mothers and daughters.

The eerie silence when they reached the scattered farm buildings increased the men's unease, that is until mocking laughter rang out behind them.

"It's drunk, they are! They've been at the brandy by the looks of things," shouted one of the women, whose sharp eyes had noticed the listless bodies slumped around the farmyard.

Suddenly many more men staggered out of the main building, outnumbering the militia by hundreds. They stopped in horror at the sight of the oncoming women.

"Mon Dieu! C'est les soldats anglais avec les manteaux rouges!" cried what passed as their leader, dropping his rifle and pointing in terror at the red shawls and tall black hats of the women.

"Oh Lord!" pronounced a bemused but smiling Lord Cawder. "I do believe they are so inebriated they think you're the Redcoats."

Alcohol induced stupor contributing to a diminishing enthusiasm for their mission, the French Capitan surrendered with little resistance, his army assembled unceremoniously from various corners of the estate to be marched or dragged to Fishguard.

This was somewhat to the disappointment of the bloodthirsty sisterhood, who followed the party.

With the exception of Jemima, who had spotted fourteen miscreants swaying down to the hamlet of Llanwnda. The other women knew better than to stop her and the men were too busy dealing with the supine relics of the French forces, as this Welsh Boadicea pursued the runaways down the hill, watching as they disappeared into St Gwyndaf's.

"Too late for praying," Jemima bellowed as she barged into the church, brandishing her pitchfork.

"Oh, I see. It's the church silver you're after, not redemption. Out of there, you bloody heathens!"

Meekly, they obeyed and with a minimum of judicious prodding were driven like cattle to Fishguard, where Jemima locked them in St Mary's Church. She then headed off to meet the returning militia.

"Bloody men! What kept you? Are there any more up there to round up?"

"Er … No Madam, I believe we have them all now." Lord Cawder uttered in bemusement.

"Well, there's a few more in the church there. I'd leave them in there overnight if I were you. Teach them a lesson. It's one thing stealing a drop of brandy and some food, another the church silver. Here's the keys. Starving I am now, so I'm off home for a dish of cawl with my man. Come on, Llewellyn."

The next day in The Royal Oak, the French prisoners officially surrendered to the local militia, claiming they had seen "troops of the line to the number of several thousand". Outside the inn a crowd witnessed the vicar make a speech praising Jemima "being of such personal powers as to be able to overcome most men in a fight" and bestowing upon her the title "Jemima Fawr" – Jemima the Great.

"That's all very well, thank you, Vicar," pronounced Jemima casting her eye over the admiring assembly, "but I see you there, Daffydd Griffiths, and you owe me two guineas!"

Charles Becker has lived in Plymouth for nineteen years, working initially as a student counsellor for the University. After retiring almost ten years ago, he joined the Plymouth Writers Group, contributing monthly short stories, and began writing for three hours every weekday morning. In 2017, he published a novel, *Murder at Royal William Yard*, through Amazon; and, in 2020, he completed the first draft of a second novel. He is also halfway through an autobiography for his grandchildren. In his earlier life he was a wine merchant and restaurateur, a gardener and an English Teacher. charles.becker@blueyonder.co.uk

Thom Boulton was Poet Laureate for the City of Plymouth (2016–2020). He is a regular performer reading at Cross Country Writers, Wonderzoo, Plymouth Language Club, and The Port Eliot Festival. Thom has been involved in projects such as the *Poppies:Wave* artistic response, a robotic poetry collaboration with *Volume AI*, has sat on the panel for the Mayflower 400 cultural bids, and co-produced a weekly poetry slot on Radio Devon during lockdown. His debut poetry collection, *Prima Materia* was published by Waterhare Press (2018), and his second collection, *Gebo*, was published by Shoals of Starlings Press (2021). Thom runs a live poetry and music quarterly event called **The Deadbeat Hotel**.

James Bridgwater's first success in writing was a couple of short stories printed in Static Movement anthologies *Comes the Night* (2011) and *Evil in Flight* (2012). Since then he has published a poems and short pieces in local anthologies. However, his real successes are his novel *Masterstroke* (2013) printed by FeedaRead.com and his autobiography *Confessions of an Emotional Shipwreck* (2016) published by Austin Macauley. He has published *Blind Justice* (2020) with Exlibris which won the Best Book in the category of Novel in Pinnacle Book Achievement Awards. It's available as a screenplay to film if he finds people to do it. www.jamesbridgwater.com

Margaret Corvid is a poet, storyteller and copywriter based in Plymouth, UK. She is a member of the Deadbeats poetry collective. Her first collection of poems, Singing In The Dark Times, is available from Patrician Press.

Lyn Douglass studied at Hornsey and Ruskin College of Art. She had 3 one-man exhibitions in Oxford and her work has been shown in Plymouth, Saltash, as well as overseas. She obtained a fine arts and psychology degree, qualifying as an art therapist in the 80s. She wrote a chapter in 'Art Therapy with Young Survivors of Sexual Abuse', "Nobody Cares" 2001. Ten years ago, she decided to write and illustrate children's books; immediately she realised her incompetency with words but soldiered on with a creative writing course and joining a workshopping group. She won 1st prize in Plymouth Proprietary Library and her work is included in 'Tothill Tales and Tittle Tattle' an anthology, 2015 as well as a contribution in The Writing Magazine. She recently finished a mural for Saltash Railway Station.

Heather Grange left school at 16. She was a mature student at university. She has won first prizes in local and national competitions and in 2013 published her first collection of poetry. As well as short stories in newspapers, two of which have been broadcast by BBC Radio Devon, Heather has read on Radio St. Austell, Cornwall and at the Torbay Poetry Festival. She has also had five short plays performed and four iPODs presented, one of which was a stage reading in the DRUM, Theatre Royal. Heather has also appeared in the People's Production of CITIZEN in the DRUM in 2019.

Alan Grant is Chair of Plymouth Writers Group. He began serious writing over 20 years ago, focusing on fiction, poetry and then progressing to material for the stage, radio, TV etc. In 2015 his short play *The School Crossing* was produced at the Drum Theatre and in 2018 a full-length play *Out The In Door* was produced by an AmDram and presented to the public over 3 days. Currently he has two plays which are currently shortlisted, one by the Kenneth Branagh Theatre Awards, and the other in a competition run by Alan Ayckbourn.

Jack Horne has published many short stories, poems and articles and a number of his poems were read on radio. Collections of his short stories, plays (written under the pen name Tucker Horne), poetry and two novels have been published and a third was accepted for publication and is listed on the publisher's website as 'soon to be released.' He won Plymouth Waterfront Writers' Jan Crocker Cup contest three times and also had some success with other contests. He was selected for a place on Papa Tango's playwriting course and is currently working on another novel.

Nick Ingram is one of the editors of *Gin City*. He is an Artist/Poet/Writer/Performer who operates out of Plymouth, England. His work is rooted in the ideas of montage, collage, cut-up, and language. Nick has published two volumes of his work: Dionysius Williams & Other Southwest Observations (2014), and Some Notes from a Small Dent of an English City (2016.) He is a founding member of Plymouth's spoken word and performance collective 'WonderZoo.' His artistic practice also extends to image making in various media and has been involved recently with local Plymouth art collective: 'Plymouth Artists Together.' Nick has published both nationally and internationally.

James Jones is 73 and lives with his wife Linda; they have four children and four grandsons. Born in Shrewsbury, he left home to join the Royal Navy. After discharge he joined the Shropshire Fire Service. While serving in Telford he became interested in performing and singing. He then moved from Telford to Weymouth. Interested in theatre he studied acting through LAMDA and gained Equity membership. He began writing and published a novel Seven Days. He has written, produced and directed a pantomime, A Town is Bourne. He writes 'Odd Odes', short sketches and song lyrics.

Merris Longstaff was born in Jamaica and emigrated to the United Kingdom in the 1960s. She started her Nursing career in the 1970s, and in recent years she trained as a Therapeutic Counsellor. She has two grown up children with her husband, Simon. As a descendant of the Windrush Generation, she has rich experience of both British and Caribbean cultures which has largely influenced her poetry. Two of her poems have been published "The Real Me", and "Black Woman". She has also written an perform her poetry in notable events, such as Black life Matters and COP 26. Her work is written and usually delivered in an authentic Jamaican Patois style, which strives to tackle the highly sensitive subjects of racism and politics around the world with both punch and humour.

Jon Mackley is one of the editors of *Gin City*. He has been writing professionally since the age of 17, working for a film company, an environmental organisation, and as an academic. He has published seven novels including *The* Gawain *Legacy, Isla's Inscryption* and *Nina's Secret* as well as chapters on English mythology and folklore, medieval and gothic literature, and edited the seven volume Spring-heeled Jack Library. He taught Literature and Creative Writing at the University of Northampton for over a decade and is Adjunct Assistant Professor at Richmond University in London where he teaches British Fantasy Literature and Early English history. Visit his website at www.jonmackley.com.

Gabi Marcellus-Temple is a visual artist, performer, writer and translator based in Saltash, just across the Tamar from Plymouth. Her practice revolves around communication and involves a many-layered approach based on extensive research and intensely immersive work. Bisexual, bilingual, bicultural and bipolar, she embraces duality in many forms and employs a playful approach to the interactions between different art forms and means of expression. When she's not trying to disrupt the status quo by pushing the boundaries of taste and open mindedness, she also works hard to promote inclusivity and diversity within the arts. https://gabipcqarts.wixsite.com/gmarcellustemple

Robin Oliver is a writer and a poet whose work covers themes of identity, belonging and personal growth within a landscape both naturally familiar and alien. He has been a member of the Plymouth Athenaeum Writers' group for several years and enjoys performing his work at live events such as Crème de la Crème. He recently wrote and performed the forthcoming LGBTQ+ monologue "Private" which was filmed and developed as part of the Write Out Loud Project. He is currently working on his first poetry collection, and would love to write a poetry comedy someday, because who wouldn't?

Pat Pettit was born in Yorkshire in 1945. After six months her parents brought her to Birmingham, her father's home city, where she raised a family, qualified as a teacher and developed a love of sailing. In 1978, her family moved to Plymouth to be with their boat in Oreston. She continued full time teaching, working in various city schools until her retirement in 1998. She joined the Plymouth U3A Writers' Group 22 years ago, writing short stories, and is Secretary of her Residents Association. She enjoys the contrasting styles of writing this involves. She no longer sails but writes instead.

Sam Richards is a composer, pianist/improviser and teacher of music. He is also a published writer of books about music and the arts. His began writing poetry seriously in 2011 and is well known as a reader at poetry evenings in South Devon. He is a folklorist and documenter of oral traditions (mainly song) in the Westcountry and elsewhere. His sound archive is now kept in the British Library. His teaching career included Plymouth University and Dartington College of Arts where he taught improvisation, modernism, oral traditions, music history, site specific projects and jazz.

Roger Schiff is a retired teacher with about 40 years' experience. He and his wife Annette have lived in the West country for 15 years. Roger is a lover of history, politics and philosophy, and is a theologian wanting to keep the rumour of God alive. He has written comic theological plays produced in a pub theatre and has recited poems at writing groups including Crosscountry Writers and Plymouth Athenaeum. He is working on a collection of poetry and history as personal reflection called "Out of Dagenham". People seem to enjoy his poetry, plays and short stories. He is currently unpublished but has something in the pipeline. rds122018@outlook.com

Chuck Jurastik – AKA Joe Vosper
Chuck was born out of the realisation that Joe had left the fame thing a bit late. He had been busy doing other things like studying and teaching but the world ignored both his learning and his teaching so his brain overfilled and leaked into notebooks which stacked up in the 60 or so hovels he'd found himself living in. Chuck and Joe have an agreement: Joe won't stop Chuck leaking when his life grinds to a halt, and Chuck won't get in the way when Joe's allowed to work. Joe is sane so that Chuck doesn't need to be. They're happy! vesperjoe@yahoo.com

Jackie Wacha is a lawyer by profession. Born in Uganda during turbulent times, her poems are about politics, human rights and climate change, subjects she is passionate about. She writes about contemporary Africa, social injustice and political change which forms the basis of her present creative practice. She has published a book about the plight of street children called Wild Rats and is currently working on her second book. Jackie is also a leading member of Waterfront Writers, a Plymouth writing group that has been going for over 25 years.

Liz Wright has enjoyed creating stories and plays ever since she could write, mainly for the entertainment of friends and family and for herself. She is fascinated by human nature so most of her stories are character driven. After her retirement a few years ago, she participated in an inspirational Future Learn course, "Starting to Write Fiction", which developed her writing skills and confidence. This led her to join a Writers' group, "Scribblers", based at Tothill Community Centre. They meet weekly during term time to vigorously workshop each other's pieces. She has also recently joined a U3A Writers' group in Plymouth. lizawright48@hotmail.com

LIST OF ILLUSTRATIONS